EARTHLY AND HEA
OF SIMONE

2002

Yang Lian *Yi* (GI 35) [China]
Lyn Hejinian *My Life* (GI 39) [USA]
Else Lasker-Schüler *Selected Poems* (GI 49) [Germany]
Gertrude Stein *Tender Buttons* (GI 50) [USA]
Hagiwara Sakutarō *Howling at the Moon* (GI 57) [Japan]

2003

Rainer Maria Rilke *Duino Elegies* (GI 58) [Germany]
Paul Celan *Romanian Poems* (GI 81) [Romania]
Adonis *If Only the Sea Could Sleep* (GI 84) [Syria]
Mario Luzi *Earthly and Heavenly Journey of Simone Martini*
(GI 99) [Italy]

Earthly and Heavenly Journey of Simone Martini

Mario Luzi

A bilingual edition

*Translated from the Italian
by Luigi Bonaffini*

With an Introduction by Barbara Carle

GREEN INTEGER
KØBENHAVN & LOS ANGELES
2003

GREEN INTEGER
Edited by Per Bregne
København/Los Angeles

Distributed in the United States by Consortium Book
Sales and Distribution, 1045 Westgate Drive, Suite 90
Saint Paul, Minnesota 55114-1065

(323) 857-1115 / http://www.greeninteger.com

First English language edition 2003
English language copyright ©2003 by Luigi Bonaffini
Introduction ©2003 by Barbara Carle
Italian edition ©1994 by Mario Luzi
Published originally as *Viaggio terrestre e celeste di Simone Martini*
(Milan: Garzanti, 1994).
Back cover copy ©2003 by Green Integer
All rights reserved

Design: Per Bregne
Typography: Kim Silva
Photograph: Mario Luzi by Ugo Zamborlini

LIBRARY OF CONGRESS CATALOGING IN PUBLICATION DATA
Luzi, Mario [1914]
Earthly and Heavenly Journey of Simone Martini
ISBN: 1-931243-53-0
p. cm — Green Integer 99
I. Title II. Series III. Translation: Luigi Bonaffini

Green Integer books are published for Douglas Messerli
Printed in the United States of America on acid-free paper.

Introduction

Mario Luzi's exceptional poetic voice stands alone in contemporary Italian poetry. He is the single poet in whom the main artistic movements and events of the twentieth century are mirrored. Since the publication of his first book of poems, *La barca* (The Boat, 1935), he has written over 18 volumes of poetry. To date there have been at least four comprehensive editions of his poetry.[1] Certainly we must not overlook his other productions, plays, poetic prose and literary criticism, and other writings. While his style is marked by a variety of distinct historical and literary periods, there are specific constants that characterize the Luzian mode in all his

---

[1] The first edition of his collective books of poetry was *Il giusto della vita*, Garzanti, Milano 1960, followed by *Tutte le poesie*, 2 volumes, Garzanti, Milano, 1979. A new augmented edition appeared in 1988, *Tutte le poesie* (*Il giusto della vita; Nell'opera del mondo; Per il battesimo dei nostri frammenti,* with an appendix of unpublished poems). Another edition followed in 1998 which included *Viaggio terrestre e celeste di Simone Martini.* In 1998 Mondadori published Luzi's *L'Opera poetica,* pp.1932, in the prestigious Meridiani series. Yet this most recent volume does not include books of poetry published since 1998.

works. In particular we note a strong lyric and visual perspective (the "heavenly" vein) which has alternated, and in the end fused, with a dialogical, recitative manner (the "earthly one"). Indeed Luzi seeks to join different voices, multitudes and at the same time, attain unity, as we may remark while travelling through the pages of this captivating and most beautiful book of poems.

Earthly and Heavenly Journey of Simone Martini[2] forms a quartet when we consider it along with Luzi's previous three books, *For the Baptism of our Fragments*[3], *Phrases and Passages of a Salutary Song*,[4] and *Sotto specie umana*, (Italy, Garzanti, 1999).[5] The four works share a similar preoccupation with light and nature. They seek to express an inexpressible absolute in a lyrical and dialogical mode.

These four books, in relation to Luzi's entire poetic opus, form his third stylistic phase. His early poetry was distinguished by a very concentrated lyric style, typical

---

[2] Original title: *Viaggio terrestre e celeste di Simone Martini*, Italy, Garzanti, 1994.

[3] *Per il battesimo dei nostri frammenti*, Italy, Garzanti 1985.

[4] *Frasi e incisi di un canto salutare*, Italy, Garzanti 1990.

[5] *Under Human Species*, not yet translated into English.

of Italian Hermeticism in the 1930's.[6] World War II had a great impact on Luzi's poetry and the books he wrote between 1950 and 1980 focused on the connections between history and art. The theatrical, dialogical and prosaic were typical of Luzi's post-War compositions. The strong dramatic vein and the intense metaphoric contrast of Luzi's early books were smoothly blended in his more recent poetry. A fluid and seemingly effortless lyricism now defines Luzi's present manner.[7]

Earthly and Heavenly Journey of Simone Martini recreates the "voyage" of Simone Martini, the famous Sienese painter who died in Avignon in 1344. Luzi, however, tells us in an introductory note that he imagined

---

[6] Ungaretti, Montale (Nobel Prize, 1975), Quasimodo (Nobel Prize, 1959) all experienced a Hermetic phase, a strongly metaphoric, compact and lyrical style which existed in the 1930's. Luzi's second book, *Avvento notturno* 1940, was perhaps the most intense expression of this manner.

[7] Mario Luzi's creativity shows no signs of waning. In 1999 besides publishing yet another major collection of poetry, *Sotto specie umana (Under Human Species)* he wrote two plaquettes, one commemorating the seventh hundredth birthday of the Florentine Cathedral, Santa Maria del Fiore, *Fiore nostro fiorisci ancora (Our Flower, Blossom Again)* and the other for Easter, *La passione (The Passion for the Via Crucis).*

the painter returned to Siena shortly before his death. The protagonists of the poems are Simone Martini, his wife Giovanna, his brother Donato, along with his wife (also called) Giovanna, and a theology student who accompanies them as witness, interpreter and chronicler of their adventure. Luzi himself is present in each of these characters, and, as he writes, in none of them in particular. The titles, Luzi adds, should function as stage instructions or captions beneath a picture or illustration. These introductory words confirm that his work has dramatic and pictorial dimensions. Characteristics of drama may be distinguished in the extensive use of interrogative forms, repeated references to another "you", of simple questions as in Luzi's previous books. The dramatic element is further emphasized by the fact that each character has a double or antagonist: Simone/Donato who are both painters, and their wives, Giovanna (one creative and sane) and Giovanna (the other, sterile and demented). Dante is named as well as his "antagonist" Petrarch. Only the theology student has no apparent corresponding other, except perhaps the reader. This opposing parallelism infuses a multitude of perspectives into the journey thereby creating a wider more all inclusive vision. Nevertheless the dialogic structure of the previous books is not as prevalent here.

While the title describes a journey, the work is not a narrative as one might expect. There are elements of the classic voyage structure in *Earthly and Heavenly Journey of Simone Martini*. The section entitled *After the Illness, Deliriums, Ravings, Visions* suggests a "shipwreck", (actually Simone's illness) and the last section entitled *Heavenly Inspection* echoes a sort of Dantesque "ascent," especially since Dante himself is addressed. Yet this "ascent" is a nocturnal fire, somewhat ambiguous and therefore more Luzian than Dantesque. Simone imagines his future "celestial death" in a dark and earthly context (the bones, the piranhas, the flesh reborn):

Empty night, plenary night.
I was not in nothingness,
though. I was
rather in being
        I thought of myself
a corpse stripped of flesh
by heavenly piranhas,
        a bone picked clean
by the dryness of winds—

            of remorse
of purification—
beneath those teeming lights,
                    when,
when, Dante,
singing alleluia for the reborn flesh?

The poems progress more towards a crescendo than an ascent. Nor can we say that the work is constructed in an "ascending" manner: Luzi's book begins ("Nature,/always uttered, named/from the origins…") and ends considering the "origins" of the word, the "advent" of creativity. Since it concludes with a question, ("Is this paradise/perhaps? Or luminous trap,/a smile of ours never conquered,/dark ab origine?) we do not attain a conventional paradise or heaven, rather a sort of delicate tranquillity, precariously, though splendidly, balanced in light.

We can ask ourselves why Mario Luzi chose Simone Martini as the protagonist for his poems. Even though he has spent most of his life in Florence and is very much a Florentine, Luzi spent the formative years of his youth and adolescence in Siena where he was immersed in the world of Sienese painting. He experienced this particular artistic tradition as a transformation and a synthesis of reality. The rapports between Sienese and French art are also important to the poet. For a long time Luzi was Professor of French Literature at the University of Florence. Therefore it is natural that he would be attracted by an Italian painter who worked in Avignon. The quest of the artist and that of the poet coincide in this book. Luzi, like Simone Martini, returns to an originary place. The question of light for the artist and the absolute mode of expression for the poet are brought together. Referring to his own book Luzi explains this poetic/artistic quest for the perfect light:

> In the last book I wrote, Simone Martini, the great painter, is called by "something," he is called to return to his origins. It's not only a question of nostalgia for his country, from Avignon to Siena, from the Papal Court to his city of painters, but it's a call to his own origins. It's a call to decipher in depth the meaning of his vocation. For he feels that there is a point art has not yet reached. He feels that art has merely reflected the world, perhaps glorifying it, but not surpassing its antinomies and contrasts. He is a great colorist and his chromatism has

enlivened Sienese painting, it has ignited it. And yet he feels that color, even though so luminous is still difference. There is, however, a light that unites everything and he wishes to paint that light, he wishes to attain it.[9]

Earthly and Heavenly Journey of Simone Martini is a chronicle of a quest for that perfect light, a form of silence and synthesis. 'Poetic painting' is a subject of representation in this book: it is the focus of the protagonist/author's reflections. Some poems describe paintings (ekphrasis) as in "Restless awakening" where Simone Martini's majestic and graceful Madonna is evoked:

But she, face flowering
the stem's grace,
dominates everything, an oval
just barely

---

[9] From *Il riscatto della parola. Testimonianze di poeti: Giudici, Luzi, Sanguineti, Zanzotto,* edited by E. Piovani and G. Porta, Grafo, Brescia 1995, p. 127. My own translation from the Italian.

granulating purple,
contains everything in herself,
seated on her throne
of peace and vertigo.[10]

Others instead concentrate on the hardships of being an artist and explicitly name several famous Medieval painters, all Masters of Simone.

Ah, we artists...
we artists are subject to many humiliations,
we have to face hardships,
the whims of the powerful, the obtuseness of people.
Even that patience is given to us with art.
The humility of the trade has never left Ambrogio
or Duccio or even Cimabue or Giotto.

---

[10] Luzi's second book of poetry *Avvento notturno, Nocturnal Advent,* was inspired by painting. For a more in depth treatment of the importance of painting in Luzi's poetry in general, see my article, *Mario Luzi's Pictorial Poesis: Avvento notturno* (1940) and *Viaggio terrestre e celeste di Simone Martini* (1994), *Italica*, vol. 73/1 Spring 1996, pp. 68-72.

In the section "He, His Art" the craft of the painter is the main focus: his use of colors, the importance of light, the various stories and persons to be depicted (The dramatic story of Holofernes and Judith from the Bible is considered and rejected). Many if not all of Luzi's other major themes are also present in this work, the incessant flow, transformation (metamorphosis and alchemy) and evolution of life is reflected in the recurrent images of light, the multiple facets of nature and reality, the contemplative or interrogative self questioning and questioning of others, and as in his earlier works *For the Baptism of our Fragments* and *Phrases and Passages of a Salutary Song,* a terrestrial contemplation of divinity.

Earthly and Heavenly Journey of Simone Martini is Luigi Bonaffini's third translation of Mario Luzi's poetry. *For the Baptism of our Fragments* (1992) and *Phrases and Passages of a Salutary Song* (1999) were also translated by him.[11] In rendering this trilogy into English,

---

[11] Other books of poetry by Luzi translated into English: *In the Dark Body of Metamorphosis and Other Poems*, tr. I.L. Solomon, Norton & Co., New York, 1975. *After So Many Years, Selected Poems,* tr. Catherine O'Brien, Dedalus, Dublin, 1990.

Bonaffini has successfully brought to light their transnational and universal qualities. He has found inventive and ingenious solutions for intricate Italian idioms and constructions. The reader may rest assured that his artful translations effectively recreate the spirit of the Italian originals.

—BARBARA CARLE

Ascolta tu pure: è il Verbo
stesso che ti grida di tornare…

Agostino, *Confessioni* IV, 11-16

You listen too: it is the Word
itself that calls out to you to return…

Augustine, *Confessions* IV, 11-16

alla città di Siena
alla mia adolescenza
alla memoria dei miei compagni

to the city of Siena
to my adolescence
to the memory of my friends

Simone Martini, secondo le storie divulgate, morì ad Avignone nel 1344. Forse recò offesa alla verità storica, forse no immaginando questo estremo viaggio intrapreso al richiamo di Siena e del suo mondo. Con la moglie Giovanna, con il fratello Donato, pittore, e la moglie di lui bella e strana, di nome anch'essa Giovanna e le loro figlie e qualche domestico si mette in cammino per l'Italia. La carovana ha da seguire un percorso lungo e faticoso. La accompagna uno studente (è da supporre di teologia) che rientra al termine dei suoi studi a Siena: testimone, interprete e cronista oltre che parte integrante dell'avventura. Lo scriba è un po' ciascuno di loro e nessuno in particolare.

I titoli fungono in questo caso da semplici didascalie.

According to known accounts, Simone Martini died in Avignon in 1344. Perhaps I do an injustice to historical truth, or perhaps not, by imagining this last voyage undertaken at the call of Siena and its world. With his wife Giovanna, his brother Donato, a painter, and his beautiful and strange wife, also called Giovanna, and their daughters and a few servants he sets out for Italy. The caravan has to follow a long and weary itinerary. He is accompanied by a student (one assumes of theology) who is going back to Siena at the end of his studies: a witness, interpreter, and chronicler as well as integral part of the adventure. The scribe is each of them a little and none in particular.

In this case the titles serve as simple captions.

ESTUDIANT

Natura, lei
sempre detta, nominata
dalle origini…
            Com'era,
come stava nella mente
degli uomini e nel senso –

                        in quel carcere, in quel
molto viva, molto cauta.   [vento,
Niente le dava, niente le toglieva il tempo.
Tempo era lei stessa, lo era eternamente.
Storia umana che le nascevi in grembo
e in lei ti consumavi
senza lasciare impronta…
                        Senza?
eppure – ma questo lo ignoravano,
non erano ancora né sapienti
né consci – entro di lei operava
                    l'universale esperienza.
E ora, tardi, se ne avvedevano in pianti.

Nature,
always uttered, named
from the origins…
           As it was,
as it stayed in the mind
and sense of men –
           in that prison, in that wind,
very alive, very cautious.
Time neither gave nor took anything from it.
It itself was time, it was eternally.
Human history being born in its womb
and consuming itself in it
without leaving a trace…
           Without?
And yet – but they ignored this,
they were neither knowing
nor conscious yet – universal experience worked
           within it.
And now, late, they realized it in tears.

Giovanna

Il rigoglio dell'essere.

                O la pena
delle generazioni.

               Forse altro
ancora me la spingeva verso
o contro.

       In quella fervida
alchimia di tutta la materia,
di tutto lo spirito,
in quella nuova numinosa genesi.
Chi era? da dove era la musica,
dall'etere o dagli inferi?

                 Fu in ansia
il cuore, pretese,
insana, di deciderlo la mente,
ancora ottusa, ancora troppo umana.
Disputa, divisione –

           sarai sempre

           e sarai sempre sovrana?

Giovanna

The flowering of being.

                              Or the pain

of generations.

                      Perhaps something else

was pushing her toward

or against me.

        In that fervent

alchemy of all matter,

of all spirit,

in that new numinous genesis.

Who was she? Where did the music come from,

the ether or the netherworld?

        The heart was anxious,

the unsound mind presumed to decide,

still obtuse, still too human.

Dispute, division –

                    will you always be

                    and always be sovereign?

Lo umilia
essere – lo sente –
cercato
    dal desiderio umano.
            Lo affligge
su di sé
    quel fiato
o quella cupidigia
d'una mente
      segugia che lo indaga
e non lo riconosce
in sé vivo da sempre –
        così spesso lo penso
        paziente e insofferente
        chi? l'unico pensabile
a me dato,
    a me baluginato
che non nomino – non oso,
come nominarlo? –
        è solo
        e sempre il mio
        io che si prolunga
con il suo patema,
temo – come nominarlo? Nomen…

Being sought
by human desire
– he feels it –
    humiliates him.

              That breath

or that greed
of a hounding
        mind that searches him
and does not recognize him
forever alive in himself
is a torture
        upon him –
        so I often think of him
        patient and restless
        who? the only thinkable one
given to me,
    glimmering before me
that I do not name – I do not dare,
how to name him? –

        it is only
        and always
        my self extending

with its heartache,
I fear – how to name him? Nomen…

Nella mente umana?

                   o nell'universo?

o in un più alto

                non distinto ibi?

È, lui,

       là,

         o è il suo mancamento?

È e non è,

          entra

ed esce dal desiderio

e dalla sua memoria,

              entra

ed esce dal nome

           e forse dall'essenza

Così li travagliava

           nei secoli

e ancora li tormenta,

           separati

essi da lui, a lui legati

da un filo oscuro

eppure rilucente

d'assenza e d'immineza.

Perché non vi guardate tutti in viso

e non riconoscete in voi la vita

dove tutti siamo?

Fatelo – supplica, mi sembra. Fatelo.

In the human mind?

or in the universe?

Or in a higher

indistinct ibi?

Is he

there,

or is it his nonpresence?

He is and he is not,

he goes in

and out of desire

and of its memory,

he goes in

and out of the name

and maybe out of the essence.

So he vexed them

through the centuries

and torments them still,

separated

from him, tied to him

by a dark thread

that yet shines

with absence and imminence.

Why don't you all look each other in the face

and recognize in you the life

where we all are?

Do it – he implores, it seems to me. Do it.

[handwritten annotation:] ibi - Egyptian glyph adviser of the gods Latin for "there"

[handwritten annotation:] Deus Abscondus in a Shiva - Like dance of absence and presence

Dentro la lingua avita,

                      fin dove,

fino a quale primo seme
della balbuzie umana? –
Discende quei dirupi lui, si cala
in precipizi
lungo venature e fibre
vibranti alcune

                    altre ossificate

da disuso e tempo.

                 Lo attirano

nel loro religioso grembo
recessi, labirinti,
pelaghi di densa oscurità
verso le infime radici,

                    fino

all'ancora muto verbo,

                  muto ma

conclamato
già, forte, dalla sua imminenza.
Ed eccolo – oh felicità – è visibile
l'altro cielo della spera
non toccato dalla creazione,
non abitato dal pensiero
ma dalla sua potenza.

                    Ed è paradiso.

Within the ancestral tongue,
                         till where,
till which first seed
of human stuttering? –
He descends those ravines,
goes down cliffs
along veins and fibers,
some of them vibrant,
                         others ossified
by disuse and time.
                         Recesses, labyrinths,
oceans of dense darkness
draw him
into their religious womb
toward the lowest roots,
                         down to
the still-silent word,
                         silent but
already proclaimed,
loudly, by its imminence.
And there – oh happiness – it is visible,
the other sky of the sphere
untouched by creation,
inhabited not by thought
but by its power.
                         And it is paradise.

Chi è - improvvisamente non conosce
costui che in vece sua
e sotto sua parvenza
subentra nel creato,
                    fende
gioiosamente con i fianchi
l'aria, le mille rifrazioni,
l'azzurra crosticina
della nuova, della madida mattina.

Lui non fu mai rigidamente lui
ma un ceppo brulicante
                    di ogni vita
immaginata vissuta
futura passata… Eppure
                    esperto
del male e delle panacee del male
                                sa
che a un punto irrevocabile
del suo peregrinare lo dirà:
«inchiodami alla croce
della mia identità
            così come fu fatto
            per te e per la tua

Who is he – suddenly he doesn't know
the one who in his stead
and under his guise
takes his places in creation,

                              joyously
cleaving the air with his flanks,
the thousand refractions,
the blue thin crust
of the new, damp morning.

He was never rigidly he
but a tree trunk teeming

                    with every life
imagined lived
future past… And yet

                         expert
in evil and the panaceas of evil

                         he knows
that at a point of no return
in his wanderings he will say it:
"nail me to the cross
of my identity

          as it was done
          for you and for yours

da cui prende dolore

e senso ogni crocifissione

ciascuno ai bracci della sua persona».

Sì, infine lo dirà:

«se inevitabile si compia».

Lo dirà, ne è certo, lo dirà.

from which every crucifixion
draws pain and sense
each at the arms of his own person."
Yes, finally he will say it:
"let it be done, if it is inevitable."
He will say it, he is sure of it, he will say it.

Quell'alone, quell'eccitato lembo,
quell'aria rilustrante
in cui balena

          la ventura primavera
ancora chiusa
nel cuore dell'inverno –

             Ritrova,
il senso, ritrova
tra sorpresa
e attesa quel mirifico
vacillamento,
ritrova lo stupore
          del ritorno
a se stessa della vita –
da dove? non ha esilio,
non ha fuga né uscita
essa – ritrova quel portento
e il suo tremore, il suo
indicibile sperdimento,
ritrova il tempo,
ritrova se stesso
prodigiosamente il senso.

That halo, that excited edge,
that shimmering air
with the glint
                    of the coming spring
still shut
in the heart of winter –
                    Sense finds again,
it finds
that marvelous wavering again
between surprise
and expectation,
it finds again the astonishment
                        of life
returning to itself –
from where? life has no exile,
it has neither flight
nor escape – sense finds
that portent and its tremor again, its
unutterable dispersal,
it finds time again,
it finds itself
prodigiously again.

L'uomo – o l'ombra –
che sul far della sera

             si volta

e guarda alle sue spalle il giorno

                       e scorge

a brani ed a lacerti
il bene
e il malefatto umano –

                ma confuso

è il profilo delle opere,

           alta l'erba

che le sommerge.

           E lasciano

macerie, murerie, carpente
sospeso un polverio.
Si smarriscono il calcolo e il criterio.
Si disorienta il cuore.
Non può fuori distinguere
né dentro se medesimo,
si perde nell'enigma
della sua specie l'uomo
o l'ombra, l'ombra e l'uomo.

               Ma

una vampa sottile li appariglia,
una sola luce li elimina.

The man – or shadow –
who at twilight
                    turns
and looks at the day behind him
                         and sees
the shreds and pieces
              of the good
and evil deeds of men –
                         but the outline of the works
is hazy,
              the grass
that covers them is high.
              And they leave ruins, half-finished brickwork,
traces of structures
a suspended dustcloud.
Calculation and criteria are lost.
The heart loses its way.
Man or shadow, shadow
or man cannot distinguish outside
or inside himself, he gets lost
in the enigma of his species.
                                   But

a subtle flame unites them,
a single light eliminates them.

Mondo in ansia di nascere…Ma stretta
è la porta dell'origine,
a miriadi si accalcano al principio;
legione si contendono
lì, al minuscolo forame,
l'entrata nel recinto,
pochi sono avviati
al caldo e alla sostanza della vita.

        Ma in epoca di grazia
        oppure d'indulgenza
          è più soffice lo sbrano,
                allora
irrompono in gran numero,
restano sì e no
un attimo sul baratro
        e subito pervadono
in tutte le sue parti il campo. Eccoli
            scendono
        l'uno
nell'altro, l'uno dall'altro, cadono
generazione entro generazione…
E noi dal gorgo
d'un oscuro tempo
lì, in quello sciame –

40

World anxious to be born… But the gate
of origin is narrow,
myriads of them throng at the beginning;
legions of them vie
for the tiny opening there,
the entrance to the enclosure,
a few are started off
toward the warmth and substance of life.
                    But in an epoch of grace
                    or indulgence
                    the tearing is softer,
                            then
great numbers of them burst in,
they remain only
for a moment on the precipice
                    and immediately invade
the field in all its parts. There they are,
                        descending
                one
into the other, one from the other, they fall
generation inside generation…
And we from the whirlpool
of a dark time
there, in that swarm –

                           fila
ciascuno il filo
luminoso
e doloroso della grande trama,
fabbrica una storia
                    nella storia
la sua cava eternità.

            each
weaves the luminous
painful
thread of the great woof,
his hollow eternity
            creates a history
in history.

La breccia che mi s'apre

         talora

per opera non so
di quale preghiera

            o di quale intercessione

nella rocca
non altera, è vero, forte
però di solitudine

         che varco

è, dove porta?
Vi penetra una parte
di me, l'attira
quel pertugio

        a una voragine

di morta

        e d'increata

fertilità.

      Mi prende

in sé quella forza,

           mi lascia alla mia sorte

l'ondata.

      Così conosco il filo

di crine sibillino

         che congiunge

separazione e unione.

The breach that at times
                    opens before me,
through some unknown
prayer
                    or intercession,
into the fortress –
not proud, it's true, but
strong – of solitude
                    that I'm entering
is a doorway to where?
A part of me
penetrates it, drawn by
that opening
        toward a chasm
of dead
        and uncreated
fertility.
        That strength
takes me within itself,
                    the wave
leaves me to my fate.
                    So I know the sybilline
thread of horsehair
                    that joins
separation and union.

Questo ardevi
ch'io sapessi?

Forse ancora non lo so? Non abbastanza?

Is this
what you wanted me so much to know?
Perhaps I still don't know? Not enough?

Simone

Dorme il suo viaggio, lui, entra
fasciato dal suo sonno
nello spazio che lo ingoia
e nel tempo che lo attende.
Entra nel suo futuro
lui, dormiente.

                  Grazia
già preparata – azzurro
e oro di un granito campo –

                               o agguato
da sempre o imboscata dell'istante –
che c'è oltre il sipario
che gli s'apre, cielo
impercettibilmente,
penombra di caverne – o niente:
il tempo a cui, figlio, si rende,
la durata a cui si affida,
il filo inafferrabile dell'universa vita…

Simone

He sleeps his journey, bundled
in his sleep he enters
the space that swallows him
and the time that awaits him.
He enters his future
asleep.

              Grace
already prepared – blue
and gold of a sown field –

                    or ever-present
ambush or ensnarement of the instant –
lying beyond the curtain
opening before him, imperceptibly
sky, half-shadows of caves – or nothing:
time to which he returns as son,
the duration to which he entrusts himself,
the unseizable thread of universal life…

Per amore di chi
                    scrive
e convive
            lui chierico vagante
            queste carte
di esilio, di viaggio?
di rimpatrio, di estraneamento…
Per devozione a Giovanna
fin dagli anni d'infanzia,
                        per avere
in pieno incantesimi dall'arte,
                            o, chissà, per sortilegio
di un artista estremo
eppure non alieno
                nella sua famiglia…
Entra ed esce dal racconto
                        stupito
d'esserne, lui, parte
al pari di ogni altro
della schiera, persona
vera, consorte, simulacro.

For whose love
                does he,
wandering cleric,
        write and live with
        these papers
of exile, of travel?
of homecoming, of estrangement…
For devotion to Giovanna
since the years of childhood,
                        to receive
full enchantments from art,
                or, perhaps, for the sorcery
of a radical artist
yet not a stranger in his family…
He enters and exits the tale
                        astonished
at being a part of it
like everyone else in the group, real
person, consort, simulacrum.

VIGILIA DI SIMONE

SIMONE'S VIGIL

Calava a picco su di lui il verdetto
o incubava nel sangue, maturava
nel chiuso della mente?
aprire ali, vele, cuori, mettersi
in movimento. Verso dove? «Dove»
non ce n'era. Luogo non esisteva.
In quel punto di luce e di fusione
veniva meno il tempo
e ogni frontiera
tra perdita ed acquisto,
tra calcolo e dispendio.
Nondimeno: in movimento!
questo era, da chi mai? il comando.

Was the verdict plunging down on him
or incubating in the blood, ripening
in the enclosure of the mind?
to open wings, sails, hearts,
get moving. Towards where? There was
no "where." No place existed.
In that point of light and fusion
time failed
with every threshold
between loss and gain
between calculation and expenditure.
Nevertheless: moving!
this was the command, whoever from?

Fermo nell'anteluce
                    immane
sopra di lui quel blocco
d'attesa e di silenzio,
gradinato dal suo verso,
scalato dal suo canto.
Non ha limite. Sempre
gli si riforma intorno, cresce
a dismisura, cuba quella montagna.
Non c'è nota così alta
che tutta la sormonti.
Storia dell'uomo
                  scesa tutta quanta
al seme, inclusa nell'embrione
della sua doppia potenza –
                              Covano
male e bene
      muti
      in sospensione, all'incrocio degli
Fermati, non spigare, non granire [eventi –
non prendere corpo
né anima – lui dice,
dice inconsultamente.
Ma eccola, lo afferra
e gli si stringe addosso
la macina del mondo. Oh, salvami.

Motionless in antelucem
            that block
of expectation and silence,
cut into by his verse,
scaled by his song.
It has no limit. That cubical
mountain reforms around him,
it grows without limits.
There is no note so high
that can rise over it.
History of man
            gone all down
to the seed, included in the embryo
of its own double power –
               Good and evil
smoulder
    silently
            suspended at the crossroads of events –
Stop, don't grow spikes, don't seed,
assume neither body
nor soul – he says,
he says rashly.
But there it is, the millstone
of the world seizes him
and presses against him. Oh, save me.

In anno domini

S'inarca, non ancora
interrogato enigma, lui nel cielo
di là dalle colline,
albica, s'inazzurra,
si apre al suo futuro, sibillino,
anno sopravvenuto,
oggi, dal suo niente.

Gli sta, colmo di sé,
ora, di fronte. Invaso
ripieno di potenza
esso, o di inanità.

Dopo la porta del dolore
le altre, successive,
del distacco, della spoliazione –
dov'è? – gliela nasconde
non sa se infinità
o, finitudine di spazio
e tempo, ma è 1à,
lo attende l'inesorabile infilata.
Varco per cui deve, ombra umana

In anno domini

It arches, enigma
not yet questioned, in the sky
beyond the hills,
it dawns, it grows blue,
it opens to its sybilline future,
year suddenly sprung today
from its own nothingness.

Now it is before him
filled with itself. Overrun,
bursting with power,
or with emptiness.

After the door of sorrow
the others, the ones that follow,
of detachment, of dispossession
where is it? – it is hidden
he doesn't know whether beyond
an infinity or finiteness of space
and time, but it is there,
the inexorable entryway awaits him.
Threshold through which he must pass,

lui pure, opacità, passare
e passerà, n'è certo,
fino al suo dilavarsi
dalle mura della città,
dalla memoria del mondo
in un diluvio di presenza
prima del sacramento
della luce, della accecante identità.

human shadow as well,
and he will pass, he is sure of it,
till he is washed away
from the walls of the city,
from the world's memory
in a deluge of presence
before the sacrament
of light, of the blinding identity.

Aderge al primo oriente
lei, prossimità dell'alba,
un suo tremore palpitante –
vittoria o resa? – non ha
esito né fine
quell'agone,

         non supera

avversario
l'avversario in quel celeste affronto.
S'irraggia, irrequietudine,
quella divina insufficienza,
ne trepida, ne brucia
pianeta o astro
la stanza, la dimora.
Vi fabbrica la storia
l'uomo, la sua illusione,
vi cuoce la sua tempra.
Perché niente riposi, niente dorma.

It rises in the first east,
proximity of dawn,
a pulsing tremor –
victory or surrender? – that struggle
has neither outcome
nor end,
        adversary does not
defeat adversary
in that heavenly contest.
That divine insufficiency
radiates, restiveness,
the place, the dwelling,
planet or star
trembles, burns with it.
Man builds history in it,
his illusion,
in it he kilns his temper.
So nothing will rest, nothing will sleep.

Guizzò una luce d'angelo
sotto la volta che non c'era

                    o era

              la fabbrica

di tutta la materia
intorno alla sua invisibile architrave.
La luce, la cercava
lui da tempo

                  essendone già invaso

in tutti i suoi pensieri
e sensi
fin sotto le palpebre – e nel viso,
raggiava nella mattina piena

                    dove lui era, di transito…

Erompe dall'oscuro
del suo scrigno
di ricordi quell'attimo e quel nimbo
o è un'immaginazione del futuro? Amen.

An angel's light flickered
under the dome that wasn't there
                    or was
                    the factory
of all matter
around its invisible architrave.
That light – he had been looking
for it for a long time
                    already invaded by it
in all his thoughts and senses,
even under his eyelids, and in his face –
was glowing in the high morning
                    where he was, passing through…
Does that moment and that nimbus
break out of the darkness
of his coffer of memories
or is it an imagination of the future? Amen.

Via da Avignone

Ritorno?
      o ripiegamento,
                un attimo
in più sicuri alberghi
dell'animo e del senso,
           effimero rientro
in terre più salubri
al corpo e alla ragione
tramutate già in splendore
      e oro dalla loro gloria?

       Saprebbero
assai meglio di lui
           rispondere
le fronti un po' aggrottate,
           gli sguardi tesi
in lontananza di Giovanna
         e dei pochi altri seguaci.
Lui esita, non sa
l'avventura che lo chiama,
non decifra l'auspicio,
         sa soltanto
che è tempo, ora, di muoversi,
    di valicare i monti.

Leaving Avignon

Return?
> or a retreat,
>> a moment

in safer shelters
of the soul and sense,
> ephemeral homecoming

in lands more wholesome
to the body and reason
already transformed into splendor
> and gold by their own glory?

> The slightly-frowning
brows, the gazes
> of Giovanna
and the few other followers
> fixed upon the distance

would be able to answer
> much better than he could.

He hesitates, doesn't know
the adventure that beckons him,
does not decipher the omen,
> he only knows

that it is time, now, to get moving,
> to cross over the mountains.

Ma intanto quello sgocciolio di tende,
stillicidio, a lungo,
nel controluce argento
degli alberi di pietra
e di quelli del bosco,

                              profusione
di tutta la materia
in unico deflusso
verso dove? L'erba là
                    all'orizzonte, aperta primavera.

                              Ma, ecco,
è in piedi la carovana,
                    attende
agli ultimi ritocchi
                    pronta – quasi –
al cammino che riprende…
                    Lui rivede
– e gli altri in sintonia?
ne dubita e lo pensa –
                    i tre giorni di diluvio
stillanti ancora
dai tetti, ruscellanti
nei fossati presso il ricovero
dove furono – perché inquieti?

But meanwhile that dripping of tents,
long trickle
in the silver counterglow
of the stone trees
and those in the forest,
                profusion
of all matter
in a single outflow
towards where? The grass there
                on the horizon, open spring.

                But now
the caravan is standing,
                it attends
to the last details
                ready – almost –
to restart the journey…
                He sees again
– and the others with him?
he doubts it and he thinks it –
                the three days of downpour
still dripping
from the roofs, streaming
in the ditches near the shelter
where they were – why so restless?

    perché taciturni? –
Così riprendono il passo,
      il varco è prossimo
lo sanno, tuttavia pare
lungo l'approssimarsi,
     lento l'ambio.
    Scoscende Falpe,
non più alpe appennino,
      casolari
qua e là, camini,
    umido
qualche furnacchio trascolora.
Smotta sotto gli zoccoli
l'appena rassoclato suolo,
slitta il mulo sopra fango
    ghiaia ciottoli,
appare, sotto,
abbagliata dalla sua baia, Genova.
O Italia ininterrotto agone,
  Ininterrotta pena.

why so quiet? –
So they set off again,
              the crossing is near,
they know it, but getting there
seems long in coming,
       the pace slow.
       He comes down the Alps,
no longer Alps now, Apennines,
       cottages
here and there, chimneys,
              some moist
smoky log changes hue.
The soil just hardened
slides under the hooves,
the mule slips on the mud
              gravel pebbles,
Genoa appears below,
dazzled by its bay.
O Italy endless struggle,
       endless pain.

Giovanna accovacciata
                    nella pausa
sotto il masso, con gli occhi
al suo già lungo tempo, sembra, fissi
a un corso tortuoso
di riviera a fondovalle
o tesi ad annullarlo il tempo
e il luogo, e ogni fine possibile
e ogni possibile cominciamento.
La include, presagisce, in sé quell'attimo,
la ingemma nella mandorla
di un perpetuante mito…

Giovanna crouching
                under the rock
during the break, her eyes seemingly fixed
upon her time already long,
upon a winding strip
of coastline down in the valley,
or fixed upon annulling time
and place, and every possible end
and every possible beginning.
That moment includes her, foresees her, in itself,
it sets her as a gem in the almond
of a perpetuating myth…

Genova, meraviglie
che a una a una sciorina –
festoso saliscendi,
sfolgorante mattino –
la nostra traversata
calando noi con ombre
in quella
solare cavità,
noi, luce, risalendo
precipizi
di pietre, ardesie, marmi,
fissa in basso la vampa
della fornace marina

      oh posta

da chi sul mio cammino,
scala, scala continua
per cui l'inferno si approssima
o il paradiso s'avvicina.

Genoa, wonders
unveiled one by one
by our crossing –
a joyful climb up and down,
dazzling morning –
we descending with shadows
into that
solar cavity,
we, light, going up
cliffs of stone, shale, marble again,
the flame of the marine furnace
motionless below
                oh placed
by whom across my journey,
stair, continuous stair
by which hell gets near
and paradise is close.

Ancora quella ambigua
luminiscenza –

               eccola
viene avanti, viene
al, centro del suo campo,
aumenta in entità,

                      cresce in vigore
di anima e di lineamento.
Visione? sì, visione
come altro nominarla?
Ma non è essa dal cuore
né dal sogno, viene
– lo sa proforidamente
lui – dal seme
di una remota antiveggenza
di padri, di sapienti. A lui
viene, perché in immagine si acclari,
perché in immagine si stampi
e rifulga il. suo lavoro
e lo smaghi e lo catturi
con le sue terre, i suoi azzurri,
i suoi ori. Oh delirio
di sovrumana grazia.

That ambiguous
luminosity again –
there it is, coming forward, coming
to the center of his field,
growing in intensity,
                    growing in strength
of soul and outline.
A vision? yes, a vision,
what else can you call it?
But it doesn't rise from the heart
nor from a dream, it comes
– he knows this deeply –
from the seed
of a remote foresightedness
of fathers, of sages. It comes
to him so it may grow clearer as image,
so it may be imprinted as image
and his work may shine
and bewitch him and capture him
with its siennas, its blues,
its golds. Oh delirium
of unearthly grace.

Petrarca

Perché non lo lasciava
un momento con lo sguardo?
Lo seguiva in ogni istante
dell'opera, scrutava
il laborioso facimento
dei volti, dei panneggi,
aspettava trepidando
la mandorla degli occhi,
dagli occhi il loro misericordioso dardo.
«Studiava il poeta della Corte
maestro in cortesia
la mia sovranità, la mia maestria,
domandava elemosina
di luce e di pietà
alle mie storie la sua arte
che non aveva storia – divorata
dalla beltà, assetata di grazia.»

Petrarch

Why didn't he leave him
a moment with his gaze?
He followed him in every instant
of the work, he inspected
the laborious shaping
of the faces, the drapery,
he awaited anxiously
the almond of the eyes,
from the eyes their mysterious arrow.
"The Poet of the Court
master of courtliness
studied my sovereignty, my mastery,
his art that had no history
begged alms
of light and pity
from my stories – devoured
by beauty, thirsting for grace."

Dormitio virginis

Primavera – piove un suo presagio,
o esala brada
caligine il suo infero. Un sentore
di future
fertilità inumidisce
il sonno in quelle giunche.
Dorme lei? S'affianca
un alto scafo,
          un'altra
latitudine si assomma.

                    Vie
strane d'acqua, non
immaginate rotte.
                Si appuntano, le sembra,
a una futura stella
              tempi aspri
a venire e tempi antichi
di remoto conio,
quell'astro li congiunge.
Perché lei? Le filtra giorno
l'oblò, s'approssima una vita,
non una vita, potenza,
quella, non docile alla forma,
immane per averla.

Dormitio virginis

Spring – an omen rains down
or its netherworld exhales
a wild haze. A scent
of future
fertility moistens
sleep in those junks.
Is she asleep? Another
hull draws up,
       another
latitude is added.
         Strange
waterways, routes
unimagined.
                It seem to her that harsh times
to come and ancient times
of remote coinage
turn to a future star,
that sphere unites them.
Why her? the porthole
filters the day for her, a life gets near,
not a life, a power,
that one, not docile to form,
immense to have it.

Ma ecco, un occhio liquido
rotante
le cerca il grembo,
la espande, sostanza luminosa
nell'universo campo.
E lei dov'è,
dov'è, ora, il suo ventre,
dov'è la martoriata vulva
della sua innocenza? Dilapsa illa
in aetere. Inestinguibile
[favilla.

But now a rotating
liquid eye
        searches for her loins,
luminous substance, it expands it
in the universal field.
And where is she,
                where is her womb now,
where is the tortured vulva
of her innocence? *Dilapsa illa*
                in aetere. Inextinguishable spark.

Notturna la sua anima s'allarma.
Dove, in che vita? È tempo
quello. Tempo ancora
e non eternità

     quel fuoco
d'acqua e luce

     dentro lo scorticato fiume.
Perché ferma alla riva?
perché? quasi le neghi
una gomena l'abbrivo,
la leghi al palo la proda.
Non si scioglie da lei
il suo passato, non prencle
ala la sua liberazione –
è questo il suo spavento.
L'avvolge invece
un misterioso grembo.
Il tempo ricordato
e quello dimenticato
e l'altro mai vissuto
da lei, eppure stato
le si stringono ai fianchi,
le scendono parimente ai sensi,
le si fondono in unità.

Her nocturnal soul becomes alarmed.
Where, in what life? That
is time. That fire
of water and light
                    within the flayed river
is still time
                    and not eternity.
Why is she motionless on the bank?
why? almost as if a hawser
prevented her from getting under way,
as if the shore tied her to a pole.
Her past doesn't get loose
from her, her liberation
doesn't take wing –
this is her fear.
Instead she's enveloped
by a mysterious womb.
The time remembered
and the one forgotten
and the other that had never been lived
by her, and yet had been,
press against her sides,
descend to the senses as well,
become one in her.

Eterno è il tempo.
È tempo l'eternità – le annunciano
i suoi angeli.

Time is eternal.
Eternity is time – her angels
announce to her.

Al centro d'una ed universa mente –
là era quel chiaro
e lui non lo ignorava. Bruma,
biancore che alonava
il ferrigno di quel monte.
Non c'è fuoco
nell'aria, c'è luce
invece e sovrannaturale pace
in tutto l'emisfero.
    E il canto,
da dove era quel canto?
a chi era cantata
    lì, nel mattino
quell'antica Messa?
Lumen de lumine,
a Dio da Dio medesimo
attraverso quella valle, piena d'assenza degli uomini.

At the center of one and universal mind –
the brightness was there
and he was aware of it. Mist,
whiteness that haloed
the steel-gray of that mountain.
There is no fire
in the air, instead
there is light and unearthly peace
in the whole hemisphere.
                And the song,
where did that song come from?
to whom
       was that ancient Mass being sung,
there, in the morning?
Lumen de lumine,
to God by God himself
throughout that valley, filled with the absence of men.

Quel viso, quella face
nel tempo.
                La copre
esso, la oscura
o improvvisamente la rialluma.
C'è, è nell'aria,
                    sface
in luce
lei la sua sostanza
                        però non la consuma.
Viso, il tuo, che prende
da ogni viso
umano, donna,
                    da ogni ramo
della folgorata pianta,
liba umori e aridità
penuria e incanto;
                        vi scende
da ogni scala
del dolore umano un rivo
di mortalità, ne è conscio.
E in questo vince,
in questa angoscia rifiorisce
immortale la sua fragifità.
Sii fermo, veglia sempre.

That face, that torch
in time,
      which covers it, darkens it
or suddenly rekindles it.
It is there, it is in the air,
            it undoes
its substance
into light
      but it does not consume it.
Your face that takes
from every human
face, woman,
          from every branch
of the tree struck by lightning,
it sips humors and aridity
dearth and enchantment;
          from every scale
of human pain a stream
of mortality descends to it,
it is aware of it.
And it wins in this,
its fragility blooms again immortal
in this anguish.
Be firm, be always vigilant.

CAROVANA

CARAVAN

Ci aspetta,
        lasciata la foresta,
                luminosa
caligine,
        laggiù quella bassura.
Bella, ma non da ravvivare infanzia
o magia
        ci viene incontro
e cangia
        una terra meno erbosa,
ci invade il senso
più fiume e meno erba
più acqua e meno terra,
ci assume in sé, ci trasporta
a un mare sonnacchioso
essa, fatta laguna.
Che fa? Ci elimina quella opaca lama?
Ci rigenera quel limo?
O è il solo
intrepido rimescolio
della vita dal suo imo, di languore
e fine con febbre di principio?
                    E noi

certi dell'esito,
questo nonostante, esito
noi stessi procediamo…
94

That lowland down there
        is waiting for us
           after we leave
the forest,
        luminous haze.
Beautiful, but not enough to revive childhood
or magic
    a less grassy ground
comes towards us
    and changes,
more river and less grass
more water and less earth
it invades our senses,
it takes us within, a lagoon now,
it carries us to a sleepy sea.
What is it doing? Does that misty swamp eliminate us?
Does that mire regenerate us?
Or is it only
the undaunted mixing
of life from its depths, of languor
and end with the fever of a beginning?
             And
certain of the outcome
just the same, outcome
ourselves, we go on…

                              Ci apre,
primavera-domenica diversa,
di svago, e di trasferta,
                         senza quasi caligine
d'un tratto
                la sua lattea incandescenza.
                         Ci schiude
la sua profondissima riserva
d'aria, d'erba,
                    fa ala
in lontananza
e in fuga
                    alla nostra
dimentica andatura
                         con lame
d'acqua, olmate,
boscaglie della sua bassura.
Ci attira a sé, ci dissolve
nel gorgo senza fondo
della sua verde accoglienza,
ci disfa, ci riforma
                    leggeri
nel suo arioso, grembo,
     madre-maga-dominica
elargitrice di assenza

A different spring-Sunday,
of relaxation and work away from home,
    almost without haze
suddenly
  opens its milky incandescence
before us.
    It unfolds
its deepest reserve
of air, of grass,
  in the distance and in flight
it lines
our oblivious pace
    with watery marshes and elm trees,
brush of its lowlands.
It draws us to itself, it dissolves us
in the fathomless whirlpool
of its green welcome,
it undoes us, it reshapes us
    light
in its airy womb,
    mother-sorceress-dominica
lavisher of absence

che ci rimette ogni debito,
ci cassa da ogni libro
e tutti ci cancella
dal passato, e dal presente.
                    Per un dopo
forse, per un ricominciamento.

that forgives us every shortcoming,
that deletes us from every book
and erases us all
from past and present.
                    For an after,
perhaps, for a new beginning.

Simone e Giovanna

Così si ripresenta lei profana
tra sogno e insonnia
del fungo dormiveglia,
così la riesuma la memoria
o il desiderio la balestra.
Viene, quasi gliela sospinge incontro
dal fondo delle sue verdi navate
una frusciante primavera

                  e lei

dentro, perduta,

          avanza

a stento e con pazienza
nel folto controvento,
però non lo raggiunge,

              le si oppongono

erbe alte, le appare
insuperabile quel campo –

              o invece la contrastano

invisibili avversari,
una forza millenaria
la trattiene, di controdesiderio
e disvolere, o altro strano, incanto.

Simone and Giovanna

That's how she appears again profane
between dream and insomnia
of the long drowsiness,
that's how memory exhumes her once again
of desire hurls her.
She comes, from the depths of its
green naves a rustling spring
almost pushes her towards him
                    and she,
within, lost,
        advances
with difficulty and patience
against the thick wind,
but she does not reach him,
                    tall grasses
hamper her, that field
seem impassable to her –
                or instead she is hindered
by invisible adversaries,
an age-old force
holds her back, of counterdesire
and unwill, or something strange, a spell.

Né lui le muove incontro
o le facilita il cammino.
Il cuore resta colmo
della sua mancanza.
Fino a quando? fino a quando?

Nor does he move towards her
or make her progress easier.
The heart remains filled
with her abscence.
Until when? until when?

Si agita Giovanna.

       Nel sonno,
agro rimorso, la mancata
maternità la affanna, procellosa
è la sua traversata verso l'alba.
Su questo non si inganna. Non gli mentono
le sue ore di insonnia
giaciglio presso giaciglio
nella ruvida capanna.

           Ma, eccolo,
le scoppia dentro
ansioso, il tempo del risveglio. Ora
non meno di lei egli si meraviglia.
È *oggi*, lo è nitidamente
in lui, fuori di lui. Eppure
da che cielo piove questo presente?
Si afferra
        la vita a se medesima,
                si apprende
ad ogni briciola,
         prolifera
si espande, avara e prodiga,
nello spazio che le è dato
o si crea
lei, si prende

Giovanna is troubled.

        In her sleep,
bitter remorse, her failed
motherhood distresses her, her journey
toward dawn is stormy.
He is not wrong about this. His hours
of sleeplessness in the rough hovel
pallet next to pallet
do not lie to him.

        But now
the time of awakening
bursts anxiously within her. Now
he is surprised no less than she.
It is *today*, it is clearly
in him, outside him. Yet from what sky
does this present rain down?
Life

    holds on to itself,

                it grabs

every crumb,

        it proliferates,
it expands, stingy and prodigal,
in the space given to it
or it creates itself, it seizes

la forza del suo fato.
Vaso d'oscurità,
bacino celeste inesauribile.
Chi lo nomina, chi gli dà grazia e persona,
donna, tu sola, a questo miracolo.

the strength of its fate.
Urn of darkness,
inexhaustible celestial basin.
Who names this miracle, who gives it
grace and person, woman, you alone.

C'è – lo sentono, lo sanno
da sempre
                per ignota scienza,
                                loro
i nuovi nati,
                un turbine nell'azzurro nembo
della loro beatitudine,
un nero in quel lapislazzulo.
Li ospita – ne sono,
oscuramente consci –
                        un'oasi, un punto
di sovrumana quiete – lì
nell'intimo e nel fondo
della vertigine perpetua.
Così scendono e salgono verso l'avvenire,
così avviene
                l'avvenire nella loro lattea mente.
Ed ecco, si condensa
la nuvola che li oscurerà,
si lascia indovinare
l'arcobaleno che li salverà.

There is – they feel it, they have
always known
                    through an arcane knowledge,
                              they
the newborn,
                    a whirlwind in the blue nimbus
of their bliss,
a blackness in that lapis lazuli.
They are darkly conscious
that an oasis shelters them,
                         a point
of unearthly quietness, there
in the core and in the depths
of the perpetual giddiness.
So they go up and down toward the future,
so the future happens
                    in their milky mind.
And now the cloud
that will darken them condenses,
                              the rainbow that will save them
can be glimpsed.

Stelle – periscono
e si formano, equilibri
nuovi si stanziano, lo sente,
sulla fine dei defunti.
                    Prati,
vigne, voragini,
là, in quelle cave
di tenebra, in quei lachi.
                    Li pensa,
li traguarda, lei, le entra
                acido nella mente
l'impolparsi celeste di quelle uve.
Letizia, turbamento.
                    Sangue il suo
che un poco si raggela,
                un po' si placa
con l'anima e coi sensi
                a quella aperta agape,
cibo costante la trasformazione
del tutto in unica sostanza,
quale? così celata dal suo nome.

Stars – they die
and form, new equilibriums settle,
he feels it, on the end of the dead.
                              Meadows,
vineyards, chasms,
there, in those quarries
of darkness, in those lakes.
                              She thinks them,
she has a glimpse of them, the heavenly
fleshing out of the grapes
                    enters her mind sourly.
Gladness, distress.
                    Her blood
chills a little,
                    it is quieted a little
through soul and senses
                    by that open agape,
constant food the transformation
of everything into a single substance,
which? so hidden by its name.

Stupore d'ultramattutina luce –
                da che
                        sonno o letargo
                                        suo
                o della specie
                                era,
                se era, quel risveglio?
niente, non si capacita il piscante.
                Deserto
gli frammischia il fiume
acqua e fuoco, gioca
col sole il suo barbaglio
ambigua la corrente.
                        Emerge
lui disorientato,
                        affonda,
                        diguazza
in quel baluginio
                        per tutta l'ansa.
                                        C'è
gli passa sulle scaglie un moto –
è appena percettibile ma c'è
in quelle acque impacciate
e in quella incandescenza

Astonishment of ultra-morning light –
               from what
                            sleep or lethargy,
                                           his
               or of the species,
                     was
               that awakening, if it was?
nothing, the being in the water cannot get over it.
               Deserted,
the river mixes
water and fire for him, the current
plays ambiguously
with the sun and its glimmering.
               He surfaces
disoriented,
               he sinks,
               he splashes
in that gleam
               through the whole loop.
                            There is –
a movement passes over his scales –
it is barely perceptible but there is
in those troubled waters
and in that incandescence

un moto verso dove? Dove corre
il moto? Il moto a se medesimo,
ci avverte, pari al tempo. Tutto cambia,
Tutto è fermo nella doppiezza del suo senso.

a movement towards where? Where
does the movement run to? Movement to itself,
it warns us, like time. Everything changes,
everything stands still in the duplicity of its sense.

S'aggronda, ma non piovono
ancora, non sfibrano la notte
e l'alba, non cantano sugli embrici,
non gorgogliano in docce
e vasi, non si strozzano agli'imbocchi
di fossi e di cunicoli, non scendono
al seme, non conturbano
l'anno nel suo cuore,
                    restano
in aria, indecise, le lunghissime
diluvianti piogge e le acquate repentine
della fertilità,
            le aspettano
erbe ancora grame
alberi, sempreverdi,
tronchi, rimasugli
stecchiti delle passate ramature.
Le aspettano – le aspettiamo,
morti, per la resurrezione.
Ogni anno, ogni ora, ogni momento.

It's getting darker, but they still don't rain,
they still don't exhaust night
and dawn, don't sing on the roof tiles,
don't gurgle into drainpipes
and bins, don't choke the openings
of ditches and burrows, don't descend
to the seed, don't upset
the year in its heart,
                    they remain
in the air, undecided, the very long
pouring rains and the sudden waterbursts
of fertility,
        grass still scanty,
trees, evergreens,
trunks, withered remnants
of past branches
are awaiting them.
They await them – we await them,
dead, for the resurrection.
Every year, every hour, every moment.

«In giorni di nubi
e di caligine»

        si oscurano

              allora

nella semitenebra le fonti,
non ammutoliscono però.

           Viene

      da loro

come dissepolto un canto
cupo

    che lentissimamente si trasmuta

     in chiarore celestiale, in squilla,

ultraluminosa guglia.

        Ha

una luce l'ombra,
una voce il nembo
nell'incommensurabile concento.
Lo sa, lui, perfettamente,
è cavata dalla roccia
del suo convincimento quella sapienza.

"In days of clouds
and haze"
      the fountains dim
in the half-shadow then,
but they do not fall silent.
          As if unearthed,
    from them
comes a dark song
        that very slowly turns
        to heavenly brightness, to bell chime,
ultraluminous spire.
        Shadows
have light,
the nimbus has a voice
in the immeasurable harmony.
He knows it perfectly,
that knowledge is extracted
from the rock of his conviction.

S'infrasca il fiume,

                    si adombra

il luccichio, si abbuia,

                    cupo liquame,

il suo poco fluire.

Scompare tutta,

           si eclissa,

ma, eccola, ne esce

solcando il nero brodo

              e, dopo, il verde nero,

                    il verde, sbuca

più oltre in pieno sole,

                lei, barca pioniera.

E ora nel diluvio

di luce,

      al fuoco,

al lampeggiare delle acquose squame

è lei che erge

la sua nera materia

controluce, nell'aria

radiosa riproduce,

pugno atroce, l'ombra.

Lo ignora o è al corrente l'equipaggio?

di quel gioco eterno

The river hides among the branches,
                    the glimmer
dims, his scant flow darkens
                    like murky sewage.
The pioneer boat
        disappears completely,
                        it vanishes,
but there it is again, it comes out
ploughing the black soup
                        and then the black green,
                            the green, it reappears
further off into the full sun.
And now in the downpour
of light,
        in the fire,
in the flashing of the watery scales
it raises
its black mass
against the light, it reproduces
darkness, a harrowing fist.
Is the crew aware of it or not?
of the eternal game

e di sé che ne fa parte?
L'oscuro, il chiaro
il loro mutuo avvicendarsi,
la storia umana, inestinguibile pedaggio.

and they themselves who are a part of it?
The dark, the bright
their mutual alternation,
human history, unredeemable toll.

Tappa e ricovero

E intanto lievemente
le monache – poche e invisibili –
preparano per gli ospiti profani,
e le aprono, un seguito di camere,
le stesse dove vissero
la regola e le vive ispirazioni
di quella plenaria solitudine
esse, e prima di esse
le altre innumerabili
che furono a quel macero
nei lunghi secoli dell'eremo

e gli ospiti serrati nelle celle
sottratte alla clausura si smarriscono
in quella vuota arnia della pura
ed infima pazienza, la riempiono
dei loro instabili pensieri
e gaudi e turbamenti…
                Alcune qui si persero,
abbuiarono qui il loro cielo
in minimi puntigli, qui si accesero

Stop and Shelter

Meanwhile the nuns –
few and invisible – lightly
prepare and open a suite of rooms
for the lay guests,
the same in which they lived
their rule and the living inspirations
of complete solitude,
and before them
the countless others
who had been in that crucible
through the long centuries of the hermitage

and the guests shut in the cells
rescued from seclusion get lost
in that empty beehive of pure
and humble patience, they fill it
with their unstable thoughts,
their pleasures and disquiet…
                Some of the nuns lost themselves here,
here they darkened their sky
with the least piques, some blazed

alcune d'acrimonie e invidie, alcune
si spartirono in letizia
tra opera e preghiera, qui bruciarono
altre una per una
le scorie dell'infelicità

                     e temprarono
lo spirito allo spirito, volarono,
alto – o il paradiso era già in loro…

Così scendono e salgono
dove tutte le storie si confondono,
in un effimero ed eternale accumulo
essi, la notte, fino all'alba, in quel profondo ricovero.

with acrimony and envy, some
divided themselves happily
between work and prayer, others
burned bit by bit
the dross of their unhappiness
                        and hardened
spirit to spirit, they flew
high – or paradise was already in them…

So they descend and rise
where all histories blend
in an ephemeral, eternal accumulation,
at night, till dawn, in that deep shelter.

Abbesse

Mente libera – parve –
uscita dalla valva
della sua cattività,
staccatasi dal ramo
del suo albero di sensi,
mente franca, intelligenza d'angelo,
suo volo, sua calata
nell'infimo
        e nel sovrumano della sfera –
chi era, non le rimordeva storia,
non le coceva identità.
              Solo era
in quel punto estasi, canto.
                    E ora

la fulmina la luce
nuova di nuove conoscenze,
le spalanca essa più nere
profondità
di non sapere. Ma è forte,
non si smarrisce, valica
i trapassi repentini
del mutevole crinale,
certa, non fosse per un grano
che le manca – lo sente

Abbesse

Free mind – it seemed –
come out of the valve
of its captivity,
detached from the branch
of its tree of senses,
frank mind, angelic intelligence,
its flight, its descent
in the lowermost
     and the superhuman of the sphere –
who it was, no history gnawed at it,
no identity vexed it.
        It was
in that point only ecstasy, song.
           And now

the light of new learning smites it,
it opens for it blacker depths
of non-knowledge. But it is strong,
does not go astray, it crosses
the sudden passages
of the changing crest,
certain, except for a missing
grain – it can feel it

e ciò le brucia – d'umiltà,
di pace, di misericordia – troppo alta,
troppo difettiva mente…

and this burns – of humility,
peace, compassion – too high,
too flawed a mind…

L'alba rese volume
e squadra alla muraglia,
al tetto il suo rossore;
confermò il recinto.
Più tardi nell'accecata vampa
s'alzò, torre di bronzo,
quella voce d'ipogeo,
chiese silenzio, pronunziò l accusa,
contro chi? Non era chiaro
chi, se l'uomo o la sua sorte.
Nessuno si mostrò.

                 Nessuno insorse
a rispondere. Rispose
una smaniosa ressa
d'ali e tube
dalla prossima boscaglia
e poi spiegato in volo
il coro vittorioso delle folaghe.
Per tutti o per sé solo?

Dawn gave back volume
and squareness to the wall,
redness to the roof;
it confirmed the enclosure.
Later in the blinded flame
the underground voice
rose like a bronze tower,
it asked for silence, it uttered the accusation,
against whom? It wasn't clear
who, whether man or his destiny.
No one showed.

        No one came forward
to answer. The answer came
from a restless gathering
of wings and coos
in the near thicket
and the victorious chorus of the coots
spread out in flight.
For everyone or for itself alone?

Dove avvallava, ora, il tetro camminamento?
Non era luogo desiderato
quello. Erano strane plaghe,
   le abitava
greve e senza voce
un pensiero altro dal suo
pieno di musica e di luce.
Perchè quel peso, perchè quella nube?
Attraversavano un pantano
di storia planetaria
senza memoria
o una piaga del creato
non compatita dall'uomo,
non riscattata dal dolore?
Di là erano gioia e festa
o là dentro era la morte?
rispondevano alterni il suo silenzio
e il silenzio, duro della coorte.

Where was the gloomy trench sinking to?
That was not a desired place.
Those were strange grounds,
                    inhabited
by a heavy and voiceless
thought other than his
full of music and light.
Why that weight, why that cloud?
Were they crossing a quagmire
of planetary history
without memory
or a wound of creation
not pitied by man,
not redeemed by pain?
Was there joy and feasting on the other side
or death within?
his silence and the hard silence
of his group answered in turn.

Acqua, notte di sotto i ponti.

                                E qui
sentori di cadavere, di antiche
putrefazioni e fiere
frollature di carni
e d'altre inconoscibili sostanze.

                             Acqua senza luce
ma acqua. Poco dopo la perfonde
il sole all'uscita dallo speco,

                             ne scintilla
essa, s'irradia
tramutata in luce, qui nell'aria,
riverbera, fiammata,
i lampi d'estate cittadina.
Oh fortuna
               di scendere accresciuta
di vita, fedele a se medesima,
sì, ma intanto con stupore
accresciuta di altri brividi,
lei luce, aria, fuoco, pura
vibrazione del mondo, culmine
               di ogni creata cosa…

Water, night under the bridges.
                          And here
a smell of corpses, of ancient
putrefaction and fierce
softening of flesh
and other unknowable substances.
                          Water without light
but water. Soon after, the sun bathes her
at the cave's exit,
              she glimmers
from it, she glows
transmuted into light, here in the air,
she reflects, flame,
the flashes of a city summer.
Oh fortune
              of descending
growing with life, faithful to herself,
yes, but meanwhile surprisingly
growing with other shivers,
she light, air, fire, pure
vibration of the world, summit
                    of every created thing…

Papillon-sombre

Ridimi – lo dice con lo sguardo
all'arcigna madre vita –
blandiscimi una volta,
una appena,
non essermi ogni giorno
ferrigna, poco amena,
       niente amica…
            così quasi mendica
luce, aria
       o briciole
di gloria dalla festa da cui è esclusa –
pensa e non s'avvede
della furia celeste che le flagra
intorno in fioriture,
fulgori di raggere,
lampi, fiamme di vigore
e la incorona
mentre vola
in piena primavera
lei farfalla-ombra, papillon-
sombre e ne fa parte,
ardore vibratile

Papillon-sombre

Smile at me – she says it with her eyes
to a dour mother life –
soothe me for once,
once only,
don't be every day
of steel to me, not very pleasant,
           not at all friendly…

                        so she almost begs

light, air
     or crumbs
of glory from the feast from which she is excluded –
she thinks and doesn't see
the heavenly fury that explodes
around here in blossoms,
gleaming sunbursts,
flashes, flames of vigor,
and crowns her
while she flies
in high spring
she butterfly-shadow, papillon-
sombre and is a part of it,
vibrating ardor,

sua anima e sua arte.
Non fruisce di sé, non trae letizia,
artista, dalla sua opera. O equità.

the soul and art of it.
She does not profit from herself, she the artist
takes no delight in her own work. O fairness.

È fermo il fiume. Sonnecchia –
amaca quelle maglie
di suoi vibratili riflessi –

                adagia

il dorso e la pigrizia
in quel meridiano sfavillio
di stelle fatue, lapilli.
Ma non è lieto,

              non ride,

come sembra

              dai raggi e dai barbagli,

                 dei suoi ozi il nume.

Gli manca, fiume,

               la sua fluvialità,

l'anima, la ventura.

                   O invece è vera pace

per lui quella pazienza

                nella stasi

e nell'estasi

          suprema concordanza?

The river is still. He dozes off –
a hammock the mail
of his vibrant reflections –

                     he lays
his back and his laziness
in that afternoon sparkle
of will-o'-the-wisp stars, lapilli.
But the deity is not happy,

                     he does not smile,
as it might seem

      from the gleams and the dazzling light,

            at his idleness.
The river misses

            his riverness,
the soul, the fortune.

            Or is that patience instead
true peace for him

            supreme concordance
in the stasis

            and the ecstasy?

Ed ecco che Giovanna, non lei, l'altra,
                    la sposa di Donato…
            Repentina
travede lei
                agghiacciata da terrori.
            In silenzio,
la sentono, tortura
immagini e memorie,
                        in sé dilania
del pari
            il vissuto ed il vivente,
                            ravvisa
insidie e mostri
                nelle povere
monotone occorrenze,
negli usati incontri,
                torcia,
ora, di demenza che deflagra
                        arida
in una maligna aria.
                    Perché, vita,
questo sfregio
che ti è fatto, ti chiedono
sgomenti. Perché

And now Giovanna, not her, the other,
                          Donato's wife…
             Suddenly
she is beside herself
                          frozen with terror.
                                     In silence,
they hear her, she tortures
images and memories,
       lived
and living time alike,
                    discovers
snares and monsters
                    in the common
monotonous occurrences,
in the usual encounters,
                    now a torch
of insanity that explodes
                    dry
in a malignant air.
                    Why, life,
this injury
done to you, they ask you
in dismay. So

crolli ogni riparo?

     e s'infrangano

limite e misura

del dolore umano? barriere

all'umana conoscenza?

      «Sia

se deve», essi pregano. «Ma passi

ad altre croci,

    presto, la nostra sofferenza.»

every shelter may collapse?
and the limit and measure
of human sorrow may shatter? barriers
to human knowledge?
"Let it be
if it must," they pray. "But let
our suffering, soon, pass on
to other crosses."

La luce che da lei declina
                    a quale altra
                    alba mira?
                                        Scolta

                    vigilia
a quale altezza di mattina
il suo sorriso che si eclissa
                    la sua mente che si oscura?
Oh nell'unico presente
perenne nascita e rovina!

The light that descends from her
        aims at
        what other dawn?
                Sentinel

and vigil
to what morning height
her eclipsing smile
        her darkening mind?
Oh in the only present
perennial birth and ruin!

Non passi il tempo, non scivoli
                    senz'ira
e senza riluttanza
                    sulle sue
nascenti rughe,
non trapassi tranquilla
e inerte nella figlia
dalle lunghe gambe e chiome
seguendo la deriva
e l'impercettibile lancetta
del desiderio del suo uomo.
Non si rassegni, preghiamo.
Ma poi che importa?
è minima la parte
di ciascuno e splendido il poema.

Let time not pass, not slide
                without anger
and without reluctance
                over her budding wrinkles,
    let her not pass calm
and inert through her daughter
with the long legs and hair
following the drift
and the imperceptible needle
of her man's desire.
Let her not give in, we pray.
But then, what does it matter?
everyone's part
is minimal, and marvelous the poem.

S'intorbida la luminosa spera,
perde azzurro, riflessi, trasparenza.
Non c'è arte nel basso, non c'è linea né forma,
non c'è pietas né umana intelligenza, ma c'è
il sangue, i suoi spaventi,
le sue furenti cupidigie.
Scende tortuosa lei, si cala
nella sua intatta animalità.

The luminous sphere gets cloudy,
it loses blue, reflections, transparency.
There is no art in baseness, there is no line or form,
there is neither pietas nor human intelligence, but there is
the blood, its frights,
its furious lusts.
She descends tortuously, she sinks
in her intact animality.

Si obnubila la mente dell'altra.
Il cammino s'interrompe. Giunge,
scagliato da quale catapulta
ignora, a lui, contro di lui l'evento.
Gli arriva come a torre
in un assedio
          un infuocato dardo.
Messaggio o offesa?
          Non ha senso
ne è conscio, la sua ira,
          è priva
di pietà quella sua angoscia
per l'impensabile ritardo.
          Eppure,
«mio Dio, perché mi provi
nel mio miserabile egoismo?»
Il geloso accecamento
per l'opera e per l'arte lo avvilisce.
È la vita nell'uomo, lo sa bene,
una ferita aperta,
          rare volte
si addolcisce
          ma non si rimargina.

          La povera

The other's mind gets hazy.
The journey is interrupted. The event
reaches him, hurled by an unknown
catapult, against himself.
A burning arrow
strikes him
like a tower in a siege.
Message or insult?
                    His anger is senseless,
he is aware of it,
                    his anguish is devoid
of pity for the unthinkable lateness.
                    And yet,
"my God, why do you test me
in my wretched selfishness?"
The jealous blindness
for work and art humiliates him.
He knows too well that life in man
is an open wound,
                    it rarely
feels better
                    but it never closes.
                    Donato's

donna di Donato ne fa prova
nei nervi, nella carne.
Lo attesta, ce lo rammenta.

poor wife lives through it
in her nerves, her flesh.
She attests to it, reminds us of it.

E ora lui si ammala.
                        Si dirama
una pazzia a lui d'intorno
in Saint-Jacques Hospitalier

And now he gets sick.
                       A madness
branches around him
in Saint-Jacques Hospitalier

Notte gli è intorno. E, sola,
                    la smania dei degenti.
Greve, più tardi, il suo
                    diurno intontimento,
                              quelle frane
del tempo, quei tracolli
della memoria entro di sé
                    e quelle braci
sepolte, non estinte.
Gli scorre sopra un fortunoso fiume
verso la foce, dice
ai suoi, verso l'anima verace.

The night surrounds him. And, it alone,
the frenzy of the patients.
Later, his dazedness in the daytime
is heavy,
those landslides
of time, those collapses
of memory within itself
and those buried
not extinguished embers.
A fitful river runs over him
toward the mouth, he says
to his companions, toward the true soul.

Nel bagaglio di Simone

Il sangue, l'assassinio –
Chi gli aveva affidato quelle carte?
perché sue non erano. Non erano
                    della sua riserva
le immagini. Non lo erano
le storie.
            Giovanna n'era certa,
                            non osava,
però, chiederlo… E se,
celata dal suo cifrato dramma,
ci fosse quella notte
biblica, quella emotività,
quella tempesta? Meglio
            non stringerlo, meglio…

In Simone's Baggage

The blood, the murder –
Who had entrusted those papers to him?
because they were not his. The images

                                  were not

from his reserve. Nor were
the stories.

       Giovanna was certain of it,

                              but did not dare

to ask him… And if,
concealed by its encoded drama
there was that biblical
night, that emotionality,
that storm? Better not to
       press him, better...

Oloferne?

Attento. Non aprire.
                    Chi suona
e dice al vocafono il suo nome
non è lei veramente,
non è colei che credi
e per antica tenerezza
aspetti
        sempre
un poco trepidando,
                    balsamo,
                              diurna
iniezione di luce e vita
                  che a te
da te profusa
            ritorna con più gaudio,

è una tenebrosa clitemnestra,
                        tiene a mala pena
celata la mannaia
che si abbatterà sulla tua nuca
schiantando testa e scheletro,
devastando in se stessa

Holofernes?

Careful. Don't open.
               Whoever is ringing
and saying her name on the vocaphone
is not really her,
she is not the one you think
and await
with ancient tenderness
     always
with some trepidation,
           balm,
           daytime
injection of light and life
that by you lavished
     comes back
to you
     with greater joy,

she is a shadowy clytemnestra ,
                  she barely
keeps concealed the axe
that will fall on your nape
splitting your head and skeleton,
devastating in herself

il tuo sogno passato,
la tua fede, la tua carità.
Non aprire! non aprire!

Ora che hai aperto dissanguati,
agonizza come deve un uomo –
ma è più di quanto
la sua animalità ricordi.

your past dream,
your faith, your charity.
Don't open! Don't open!

Now that you have opened bleed to death,
agonize as a man must –
but it's more than
                              his animality remembers.

Nera croce a cui era
inchiodato per mano di sicario
e di proditoria amante.
Aria… dov'era
l'aria? Non ce n'era
sotto il cielo,
non vigeva, lei,
aria, in nessuna plaga.
Rientrata nelle crepe,
riassorbita dai pori
della mura e della pietra?
Non c'era l'aria, c'era
la totale mancanza
di lei e del respiro
della vita ritirata
nel buio delle viscere,
risucchiata dal gorgo
della perdita. Forse dell'origine.

Black cross to which
he was nailed by the hand of a cutthroat
and a treacherous lover.
Air… where
was the air? There wasn't any
under the sky,
the air wasn't strong
in any region.
Gone back into the crevices,
reabsorbed by the pores
of the walls and of the stone?
There was no air, there was
the total lack
of it and of the breath
of life withdrawn
into the darkness of the viscera,
sucked back by the whirlpool
of the loss. Maybe of the origin.

La donna del sicario
che qui era di casa
come amata e come figlia
involgarita nell'anima,
profanata nella carne
disarma il desiderio,
devasta fede e sogno.
Ma attento! guardati, ti prego:
essa, buio rottame,
galleggia in una broda
di mezze verità e di menzogne,
t'insidia con calcolato affetto,
conta, oh non a torto, sulla tua
creaturale carità. Guardati, guardati!

The cutthroat's woman
who was at home here
as loved one and as daughter
made vulgar in the soul,
violated in the flesh
disarms the desire,
devastates faith and dream.
But careful! watch yourself, I beg you;
she, dark flotsam,
floats in a swill
of half-truths and lies,
she ensnares you with calculated affection,
she counts, oh not without reason, on your
creatural charity. Watch yourself, watch yourself!

Via, chiudere nell'involucro quei fogli,
fissarli nel fermaglio, allontanarli
da sé. Arriva il far del giorno,
a gara si alternano le aubades.
Le ascoltano tutti, unificati dal canto.

Come on, let's put away those sheets inside the folder,
let's paper-clip them, remove them.
The break of day is coming,
the aubades *are competing with each other.*
Everyone is listening to them, unified by the song.

Lied-aubade

Ma tu dimmi, ti prego,
perché tarda
            tanto l'alba.

                        Dove
sono,
        non li sento
ancora,
            quei rari
                    che dichiarano:
è giorno, e ne ripetono
l'annundo, e ne ribattono
forte
        il conio da selce a selce
allegramente scarpinando…
Non li sento, non ci sono.
E gli uccelli persi
nell'universo loro, muti,
                        fino a quando?

Lied-Aubade

But you tell me, I beg you,
why dawn
      is so late.
                Where
are,
      I still can't
hear them,
      those rare passers-by
            who declare:
it's daylight, and they repeat
the announcement of it, and loudly
beat its coin
      from stone to paving stone
cheerfully tramping…
I don't hear them, they are not there.
And the birds lost
in their universe, silent,
                till when?

Primo cantore

Primo,
     unico
          in tutto il circostante
spazio,
tempo – infigge la primizia,
il canto;
     in tutto il cavo
     inabitato argento
lo ribatte
       finché esce la luce
dal suo incanto, cresce,
si diffonde
       e allora sul suo esempio
         alcuni,
altri per discordanza
bruciano l'armonia nascente,
         sfibrano,
con febbre ed ingordigia
quell'indicibile sostanza…
     Ma c'è,
come ignorarla? È svelata.
E come ritrovarla?
       L'aspetta
il giorno, tutto il tempo della prova.

First Singer

First,
        the only one
                        in everything around –
space,
time – plunges in the first fruit,
the song;
        in all the hollow
        inhabited silver
he rivets it again
        until the light comes out
of its enchantment, grows,
spreads
        and then, following its example,
                            a few,
others, burn the new-born harmony
in discordance,
                        they exhaust
that inexpressible substance
with fever and with greed…
        But it's there,
how can it be ignored? It's revealed.
And how to find it again?
                        The day
awaits it, the whole time of the trial.

Matura essa, macera, assottiglia
fino alla più luminosa
        inesistenza-essenza.

It ripens, it wears down, it thins
to the most luminous
               inexistence-essence.

Perché nascere ancora? –
sembra si rivolti il giorno –

a illuminare che scempio
oppure che tripudio
                          nell'eterna
universale alternanza?

Perché? – quasi s'incorna,
giorno recalcitrante
alla dura norma…

Rompe la fedeltà
a quell'alto tedio –
non c'è precorrimento
di canto nella smania degli uccelli,
non c'è acume vigilante
nei pensieri degli insonni

ma sale, giorno nuovo,
giorno prima mai visto
sulla cresta del tempo
al lavoro necessario.

Why be born again? –
the day seems to rebel –

to illuminate what havoc
or what rejoicing
                in the eternal
universal alternation?

Why? – it almost digs its heels,
day bucking
at the hard rule…

It breaks faith
with that high tedium –
there is no presage
of song in the birds' restiveness,
there is no vigilant insight
in the thought of the sleepless

but it rises, new day,
a day never before seen
on the crest of time
to do its necessary work.

Alba, quanto fatichi a nascere!

                         Ti tiene
                         alcuno

stretta
      al suo nero impedimento,
non vuole tu ti sciolga
la notte
      dal suo buio grembo.
O sono io non pronto
                ancora
al tuo miracoloso avvento…
Ti aspettano con me –
lo sento – i profili montuosi,
le cime,
      i precipizi
               del luogo e della mente
nella plebe degli insonni
               e anche
nelle gallerie dell'anima
               ed in quelle
di Siena e di Firenze
         le immagini e i dipinti
ansiosi di risplendere
            e le acque

Dawn, how difficult is your birth!
                    Someone
                    is keeping you
tight
        in his black impediment,
he doesn't want you to get loose
from night's
        dark womb.
Or am I not ready
                    yet
for your miraculous appearance…
Waiting for you with me –
I feel it – are the outlines of the mountains,
the peaks,
        the chasms
                    of the place and of the mind
in the sleepless masses
                    and also
in the galleries of the souls
                    and in those
of Siena and Florence
                    the images and paintings
anxious to shine brightly
                    and the waters

che aprono
il loro borbottio notturno
a un più vetrato
e cristallino canto
e gli uccelli
che smaniano e non tengono
nella gorga il loro verso,
tutti,
alba, ti aspettiamo
sapendo e non sapendo
quel che porterai con te
nella tua ripetizione antica
e nel tuo immancabile
antico mutamento…

that open
their nocturnal murmur
to a glassier
more crystalline song
and the birds
that fidget and can't keep
their cry inside their gullet,
all of us,
dawn, are waiting for you
knowing and not knowing
what you will bring with you
in your ancient repetition
and in your inevitable
ancient transformation…

Quel vegliardo che quasi quasi danza
e senza toccarlo lo solleva
dalla sua buia lacuna –
La notte porta quel sogno,
lo porta ripetutamente.
Con volto sempre più puntuto,
con libri sempre più segreti
lo attira in quell'abisso
della sua troppa luce,

              gli apre,

                  lui

che pure n'è accecato
una scoscesa porta
per cui l'uomo è passato

              solo prima.

Prima di esserlo.

            E che *dopo*

divenuto umano
finalmente ritroverà.
Dice questo in un sussurro,
ma non quando sarà.

That old man who is almost dancing
and without touching him lifts him
from his dark recess –
Night brings that dream,
it brings it repeatedly.
With a face ever more pointed,
with ever more secret books
he draws him into the abyss
of his excessive light,

                        he opens for him,
                             although

he himself is blinded by it,
a steep door
through which man has passed
                        just before.

Before being a man.

          And that *after*
becoming human
he will finally find again.
He says this in a whisper,
but not when it will be.

DOPO LA MALATTIA

DELIRI, VANEGGIAMENTI, VISIONI

AFTER THE ILLNESS

DELIRIUMS, RAVINGS, VISIONS

Sole, lei, si leva
in cielo aperto
                    da molta oscurità,
                            da troppo
spessore di caligini.
                            Quale cristallo,
quale limpidezza umana
ne riflettevano il fuoco,
lo captavano dentro il loro impasto!
Così ricordava le sue estasi
in quella dei suoi supplici…
Ma, ecco, è lei che scende quella scala
e penetra ostinata
                    quella oscurità tapina,
ne visita le tane
di vizio e di dolore,
                        ne deliba
i veleni d'idiozia,
                    la nera
quintessenza di perfidia.
La luce non le pare luce
se non piena di tenebre,
la sua letizia non sarebbe lieta
senza la condivisa pena –

She, a sun, rises
in the open sky
               out of deep darkness,
               out of the thickest
shadows.
               What crystal,
what human transparency
reflected her fire,
captured it within their mixture?
That's how she remembered her ecstasies
in that of her supplicants…
But there now, it is she who is descending that stair
and stubbornly enters
               that wretched darkness,
she visits its dens
of vice and pain,
               she relishes
its poisons of idiocy,
               the black
quintessence of treachery.
Light does not seem light to her
unless filled with shadows,
her joy would not be joyful
without the shared hurt –

cantano lodi antiche…

                    Ma è
quell'infelicità che cerca, pascolo
alla sua misericordia o elemosina
                    che chiede?

Elemosina celeste?

they sing ancient praises…
                              But is it
that unhappiness she is looking for, grazing ground
for her compassion, or is it alms
                              she asks?
Heavenly alms?

Si leva, quasi un alleluia, lei
nell'alba. È ilare,
già apre, già ravvia la stanza,
scompagina coperte
e coltre – e sfodera
e sprimaccia
            il guanciale del suo sonno.
Presto, prima che il sole
entri e le perquisisca il nido,
                    spazza
ricordi e sogni
sospesi a brani –
            ricordi
o sogni? ormai
non li discerne
la mente già diurna,
nondimeno li riattizza
tutti e tutti li sfruculia…
Vita che ad altra vita
pietosamente umilia
perché il giorno nasca puro
e ignaro e pieno di sapienza –
Sorride, lo sappiamo,
di questo il suo sorriso;

She rises in the dawn,
almost an alleluia. She is cheerful,
she already opens and tidies up the room,
she tousles blankets
and cover – and takes the pillow of her sleep
                              out of its case
and fluffs it.
Early, before the sun
enters and searches her nest,
                              she sweeps
memories and dreams
suspended in shreds –
              memories
or dreams? now
the already diurnal mind
does not discern them,
and yet rekindles them
and stirs them.
Life that mercifully
offers itself to other life
so the day may be born pure
and unaware and full of knowledge –
Her smile, we know,
smiles at this;

di lei compagna o figlia
a cui siamo affidati
eternamente strapazzata ciurma
finché ci porti in salvo,
finché ci annulli.
Nel principio, nella sorgente.

at herself as mate or daughter
to whom we are entrusted,
throng eternally ill-treated,
until she rescues us,
until she annuls us.
In the beginning, in the wellspring.

Dov'era *lui?*

   dietro la maschera caduta
non c'era il suo né alcun altro volto,

     c'era,

anonima e indistinta,
una dura non-figura
scavata dalle ère,
modellata dagli eventi.
Non un alibi, non una
disertata faccia —

   prega,

se mai una più intima colata
di umano e di divino
nell'universo plasma
che ora s'incendiava
sopra, nella luminosa volta.

Where was *he?*

behind the fallen mask

there was neither his nor any other face,

there was,

anonymous and indistinct,
a hard non-figure
dug by the ages,
shaped by events.
Not an alibi,
not a deserted face –

he prays for,

if anything, a more intimate pouring
of human and divine
in the universal plasma
that now was catching fire,
above, in the luminous vault.

Le scende per le braccia
ai fianchi, si diffonde
in tutte le membra quella fresca
e festosa mattutinità –
Lei avanza contro sole,
                    s'immerge
in quella tempra
                    abbrivida,
ancora duro intoppo,
le sembra,
al dilagare della luce
                    finché, ecco
le entra il mondo
nei sensi, nella conoscenza.
È lei che traversa quella nube
o è quella nuvola cangiante –
la vita -– che la invade
e tutta la percorre?
                    chi è l'ombra?
                    chi è che lo decide?
Oh niente, niente, lo sai bene, le distingue,
se non la nostra allarmata insufficienza.

That fresh and festive morningness
descends through her arms
down to her flanks, it spreads
throughout her limbs –
She advances against the sun,

                        she plunges

into that hardness,
              she shudders,
still a hard snag,
it seems to her,
at the flood of light
              until
the world, now, enters
her senses, her consciousness.
Is she going through that cloud
or does that changing cloud –
life – invade her
and run all through her?

                  who is the shadow?
                  who is it that decides?
Oh nothing, nothing, you know it well, distinguishes them,
other than our frightened insufficiency.

Non ancora il radioso degli alberi
delle siepi, dei cespugli.
Non ancora, ma presto,
domani forse
nel rilucere dell'erba
un fulgore di forsizia,
l'allucciolo del fiume
                    torno torno
alla pigrizia delle barche.
Fedeli, ma con nuova meraviglia,
al loro appuntamento
la natura e il senso.
Domani, domani, già ora, guarda!

Not yet the radiance of the trees,
of the hedges, of the bushes .
Not yet, but soon,
maybe tomorrow,
in the glitter of the grass
a brilliance of forsythia,
the shimmer of the river
                all around
the laziness of the boats.
Nature and sense
faithful to their appointment,
but with new wonder.
Tomorrow, tomorrow, already now, look!

Ti prego, non ritornino.

                        Ore
di carcere in cui ero
in compagnia di me
che m'ero inviso
per nero disamore
e tu non eri e non venivi
in visita o a dimora
come immagine o come memoria
o in forma di preghiera –
ore cieche, ore nere
in cui era penuria
d'aria, più ancora di colore
e non c'era né ardore né pittura…
Più tardi, quando da evaso
di quella prigionia
mi riversai, mi espansi
in molte simiglianze, in molte
fraternità, forse mi avevi
invaso, ma io non lo sapevo
e non potevo, altri
ero, non io, quel ricongiunto
con la fulgida agonia
del mondo e delle sfere.

I beg you, don't let them return.

                              Hours
of imprisonment in which I was
in company of myself
to myself hateful
through black disaffection
and you were not there and did not come
to visit or to stay
as image or as memory
or in the form of prayer –
blind hours, black hours
in which there was little
air, even less color,
and there was neither ardor nor painting…
Later, when fugitive
from that prison
I poured, I expanded
into many resemblances, into many
brotherhoods, perhaps you had
invaded me, but I did not know it
and could not, I was
someone else, not I, the one reunited
with the brilliant agony
of the world and of the spheres.

Né tu eri la stessa
della tua mancanza,
nessuno era più niente, luce,
luce regina solamente.
Così era, così sia sempre.

Nor were you the same
as your nonpresence,
no one was anything now, light,
light queen only.
So it was, so may it be always.

Di che questa penuria?

                           di che manca

il cuore

            che quasi non respira?

                           d'aria

e luce?

      di canto?

Chiuso, sotto la mole

non sa se della storia

umana o di che altro evo,

brucia, consuma

solo un poco

                il tempo

della sua

            interminabile contumacia.

Oh poco. Troppo poco – pensa.

What is this lack of?
              what is the heart
missing
      that it almost cannot breathe?
                              air
and light?
      song?
Shut under the bulk
it doesn't know whether of human
history or of what other age,
it burns, it consumes
only a little
      of the time
of its endless truancy.
Oh, little. Too little – he thinks

Guardalo, si dona.

              Non staccarlo

però, dal ramo,

           lascialo che penda

al sole e all'ombra

tra il fogliarne   e assuma l'aria

la luce, la stagione.

Piace la sua maturità

al pomo, a te la voglia

non dispiace. E bruciano in accordo.

Look at it, it offers itself.
                    But don't detach it
from the branch,
                    let it hang
in the sun and the shade
amid the foliage   and let it take in the air
the light, the season.
The fruit likes
its ripeness, you don't mind
the craving. And they burn in unison.

In acqua e in aria
cangiando d'ora in ora
                    trepidò
nei suoi fulgori
               la città dov'era –
Venezia? non in sogno? vera? – stette
lui abbacinato
                dal tripudio
                           visibile
invisibile presente in ogni dove
dei riflessi, delle trasparenze
e da come lo falciavano
netto, a volo teso i colombi,
lui? o di lui una
già postuma
                incandescente spera
                erratica nel tempo –
ma c'era il tempo, la morte?
                              o c'era
l'ininterrotta danza
dell'essere che aveva ora d'intorno
in lunule e baleni
e non altro da lei
                senza confini
                né porte?

In water and air
changing hour after hour
                    the city he was in
quivered
        in its splendors –
Venice? not in a dream? real? – he was
dazzled
        by the visible
invisible everywhere present
revelry of reflections, of transparencies,
and how the pigeons
cut clean across it
in their taut flight.
he? or an already
posthumous
                    incandescent sphere of him
                    wandering through time –
but was there time, death?
                        or was there
the uninterrupted dance
of being that now he had around him
in lunules and flashes
and nothing else from it
                    without bounds
                    or doors?

S'ammassa Roma, raggruma
il vasto polpo
in un brunito corno.

           E sopra e contro,
           un brivido, il celeste
           e il rosa dell'estremo addio del
Non si perde, lo colgo   [giorno.
che si figge, quell'attimo,
negli occhi, nere prugne
appena opalescenti,
di lei madre matuta
degli ininterrotti tempi
che ai piedi della mura
mi sceglie ora, m'incarta
con ritmo e con pazienza
i minimi garofani –
suo inverno – e aggiunge
con un suo sorriso
           l'offerta delle mammole
raccolte in quale averno?
     Ed eccolo, mi venta in volto
l'ignoto che lei sa, da sempre,
mi splende incontro l'assidua
minifabbricazione della morte

Rome crowds together, it clots
the vast octopus
into a burnished shell.

    And above and against,
    a shiver, the pale-blue
    and the violet of the day's final farewell.
That moment does not get lost,
I catch it as it transfixes
her eyes, black prunes
barely opalescent,
she mother matuta
of uninterrupted time
that now chooses me
at the feet of the walls,
wraps the smallest
carnations for me
with rhythm and patience –
her winter – and adds
with a smile
  the offer of the violets
gathered in what avernus?
  And there it is, the unknown
she has always known
blows in my face,
the assiduous minifabrication

che in vita si converte. O Rom.

of death converting into life
shines toward me. O Rom.

Tra i monti tale e quale
quella celestiale calma.
                    Identica
nel ritmo quella danza
di ore, voli,
              martellanti suoni.
E ancora a Macerata,
in Osimo la rapinosa ruota,
                        l'infuriante
                saliscendi
di rondini
              attorno ai campanili
sopra i tetti
              le cupole
                    le altane.
Oh tempo che a te stesso ti parifichi
e ti arrendi alla tua
imperante eternità,
non dimenticarti degli uomini,
              non li gettare ai tuoi margini.

Among the mountains that heavenly
calm is always the same.

                    Identical
in the rhythm that dance
of hours, flights,

                    hammering sounds.
And again in Macerata,
in Osimo the whirring wheel,

                    the furious
to and fro
of swallows

        around the belfries
above the roofs

                    the domes

                    the roofterraces.
Oh time that make yourself equal to yourself
and surrender to your
ruling eternity,
don't forget men,

                    don't cast them off at your edges.

Tentavano l'aria,
stormivano fogliando
esse, mani di donna
        al vento del futuro incontro…
Non era per diletto,
                andavano
ciascuna ad una prova,
tutte al mondo,
a intesserne la trama,
                a riammagliarne
i logorati fili,
        io stame in quella tela
il tempo loro
e il mio a fatica interpretando…
Come sorte? Come sorte e come grazia…

They grazed the air,
they rustled as they leafed,
woman's hands
        at the wind of the coming encounter…
It wasn't for pleasure,
                each of them
was going to a trial,
all toward the world,
to weave its web,
                to knit together
its worn threads,
                I a fiber in that cloth
struggling to interpret
their time
and mine.
As fate? As fate and as grace…

E gli aromi?
   d'aromi unico il tuo
   dolcissimo e furente,
      estate che ora nasci
nel gelsomino e nel tiglio
     e cresci forte,
       dilani
la primavera
   ai suoi ultimi ritardi
   con la mischia
ormai senza quartiere
di effluvi e di sentori –
    celeste
e nauseabonda
   su cui delirano le rondini
   e anche la mia insonnia…
Eh che importa il malaticcio
che intanto le opaca l'incarnato
e le riduce i bei capelli in pania?
Che importa? È vivo quell'aroma
in noi come lo fu quel giorno
… quale? La memoria è vana.

And the aromas?
     your unique aroma
     so very sweet and raging,
               summer that now is born
in the jasmine and lime tree
          and you grow strong,
                you rend
the spring
     in its last pauses
          with the melee
now without quarter
of fragrances and scents –
          heavenly
and revolting
          over which swallows rave
          and my insomnia as well…
Ah, what does the sickliness matter
that dulls her rosy flesh meanwhile
and turns her lovely hair to birdlime?
What does it matter? That aroma is alive
in us as it was that day
…which? Memory is useless.

Non ha senso l'istante. Ne ha il tempo,
ne ha la misteriosa
continuità di esso – pensa.
È ora, o quando?
è sempre.
          Nella via
del ritorno
          si diradano i paesi
terre, nuvole, montagne…
la stretta al cuore
li strugge
tutti, l'uno nell'altro
i suoi settembri,
la loro mutevole agonia
di luce, d'aria,
di origini e memorie,
memorie nel ricordo, memorie
perse al ricordo… O caos celestiale.

The instant has no meaning. Time does,
so does its mysterious
continuity – he thinks
Is it now, or when?
it is always.
         On the way
back
         the towns, the lands,
the clouds, the mountains thin out…
the heartache
consumes
all, one in the other
his Septembers,
their changeable agony
of light, of air,
of origins and memories,
memories in remembrance, memories lost
to remembrance… O heavenly chaos.

SIMONE E IL SUO VIAGGIO

SIMONE AND HIS JOURNEY

Vibrò,
      etere fuso
              nella trasparenza
      dell'aria
           di luglio
                  la mattina, esplose
nell'azzurro fuoco
e subito fluì
           nel mediocielo il trillo.
          Si aprì a quel richiamo
il cuore, sì,
        e lo patì, stilo di lutto
e d'ansia.
          Ma entrava nella stanza
e nell'infermo,
             che ero gioia e spasimo
del ricominciamento
di sé da sé del mondo
e della fonte, macula
io e impurità,
          di quel travaglio parte,
          di esso accidentale
o previsto messaggero.
Luce s'illuminò da luce,
fu ogni oscurità, la mia non meno,
abbagliata fino a quando… oh verità…

The morning
        quivered,
                ether fused
        in July's
                transparency, it exploded
in the azure fire
and suddenly the trill
        flowed in mid-sky.
        The heart did open
at that call,
        and suffered it, dagger of mourning
and anxiety.
                But it entered the room
and the sick man,
                I who was joy and spasm
of the new beginning
of itself from itself of the world
and of the source, I macula
and impurity,
                part of that labor,
                accidental
or foreseen messenger of it.
Light was illumined by light,
every darkness, mine as well,
was dazzled until when… oh truth…

Forte. Forte la luce
e già penetrata in ogni dove
                    nel più folto del fogliame.
Non ci fu vento né boria.
                    L'unisono s'infranse
                              si tritò
                              in briciole
di minima vetriglia
                    prima l'infima
poi la superna
cristalleria del canto.
Sgomento.
                    Poi cantò da solo il giorno
nel suo fulgore dilagante.
Cantò nell'ima mente
nel sangue e nelle vertebre
degli uomini al lavoro
fin dall'alba. Cantò
se stesso e in sé tutta la storia
senza parti, senza memoria.

Strong. The strong light
has already penetrated everywhere
                    into the thickest foliage.
There was neither wind nor vainglory.
                              The unison shattered
                              it splintered
                              into crumbs
of minute bits of glass
                    first the lowest
then the highest
crystal note of song.
Dismay.
                    Then the day sang by itself
in its flooding radiance.
It sang in the lowest mind
in the blood and the vertebrae
of the men at work
since dawn. It sang
itself and in itself all of history
without parts, without memory.

Le prode verdi, il flusso d'acqua e luce,
gli alberi trepidanti sulla mia
solitaria sgambatura…

                        E voi tutti presenti,
miei cari, tanto da dimenticarvi.
Talora «è questo il paradiso» penso
nella mia traboccante gratitudine –
«O un suo irrefrenabile lampeggiamento.»
(Suo, della sua eternità o del suo attimo)

The green shores, the flux of water and light,
the trees quivering on my
solitary trek…
             And all of you present,
my loved ones, to the point of forgetting you.
At times "is this paradise" I think
in my overflowing gratitude –
"or one of its uncontrollable flashes."
(Of it, of its eternity or of its instant).

Leone.

    Nell'aria quel nerore.

          Muto
alle vigne sdirupa l'incasato.
Sonno o grevità

        di sangue e di pensieri

          li attanaglia
questi,
questa tribù
dura, acquattata
che la calura cuoce
nelle tane, nelle mura,

        uomini
pure, ciascuno

      con mire e desideri.

      Dove errano,
dove puntano
i desideri, i loro?

      E quegli che laggiù
da sotto quegli embrici la mira…
Gli legge nello sguardo
le sue truci voglie.
Che parte torba,

     che misera porzione

Lion.
      That blackness in the air.
                      Mute
the group of houses plunges toward the vineyards.
Sleep or heaviness
            of blood and thoughts
                        clutches them,

this hard
tribe, crouching,
that the heat scorches
in the lairs, inside the walls,
            yet
men, each
      with goals and desires.
            Where do their desires
wander, where do they aim?
            And the man down there
looking at her from underneath those roof tiles...
In his gaze
she reads his savage lust.
What a murky part,
            what a shabby portion

del fuoco e della danza
a lui tocca – dice
        calmo il viso di Giovanna. E prega.

of the fire and the dance
is given to him – Giovanna's face
                    says calmly. And she prays.

Durissimo silenzio
tra noi uomini e il cielo,
                              arido
per aridità di mente

o scomparsa degli angeli
rientrati nel Verbo, muti,
alla sorgente,
                    afasia, anche,
o morte dei profeti,
                         ma colmato
da nuvole, da pietre,
da alberi, animali,
                         da quel loro
ininterrotto afflato,
                    tutto, creaturalmente.
O anima del mondo,
da tutto ferita,
da tutto risarcita,
non piangere, non piangere mai –
                              dice nel sonno
la sua amorosa lungimiranza.

Very hard is the silence
between us men and the heavens,
                              barren
through the barrenness of the mind,

or the disappearance of the angels
gone back into the Word, silently,
to the source,
        aphasia, also,
or death of the prophets,
                  but filled
with clouds, stones,
trees, animals,
                  by their continuous breath,
                  completely, creaturally.
O soul of the world,
wounded by everything,
compensated by everything,
do not weep, never weep –
                  his loving
farsightedness says in his sleep.

Ira
dura, sgomento. L'essere
tra il sì e il no
nel mediodìe s'infranse.
In bilico tremò la persistenza.

                Soffrì

storia dell'uomo,
delle specie, delle stirpi,

                   genìa cieca

colpita nel midollo,
offesa nel seme, nelle vertebre.

               Soffrì,

senza pedaggio
di storia e di sudario
dalle sue perdute origini
e agonie il cosmo
esposto a quel ludibrio,
inalzato a quel silenzio
di pece, di lapidario.
Così lo preparava
lui in angoscia – ne sfaceva
già il pigmento
in animo, in potenza –
il terribile dipinto

Hard
anger, dismay. Being
between yes and no
in midday shattered.
Persistence trembled in the balance.
                    The history of man,
of the species, of the races suffered,
                    blind tribe
struck in the marrow,
offended in the seed, in the vertebrae.
                    Without toll
of history or sudarium
from its lost origins
and agonies the cosmos
suffered
exposed to that jeering,
raised to that silence
of pitch, of stone-pit.
So he was preparing it
in anguish – and was already undoing
its pigment into soul, power –
the terrifying painting

del dolore, della vittoria,
lui uomo dalla croce
della umana continuità.

of sorrow, of victory,
the man from the cross
of human continuity.

San Sebastiano

Frecce.
      Sentiva lui malgrado
            quel male acuto del costato,
                  freece
            ronzare ancora, spingersi
l'una dopo l'altra
            vibrando sul bersaglio
e il bersaglio era il suo fianco.
Nella sua prossimità
            sviava
ecco qualcuna,
            sviavano
in molte, l'una dopo l'altra
verso quale altro destino…
Lui è al centro
della sofferenza, è posto
ivi, onfalo
lui medesimo del male,
della tortura.
            Perché io, perché
questa acrimonia
del nemico
            contro le mie carni?
Monotono demonio.

Saint Sebastian

Arrows.
      Despite that sharp pain in the ribcage
          he still felt arrows
               whir, hurtle
one after the other
      vibrating toward the target
and the target was his flank.
A few of them
      strayed next to him,
many of them strayed, one after the other
toward what other destiny…
He is at the center
of suffering, he is placed
there, he himself
omphalos of the pain,
the torture.
      Why me, why
this acrimony
of the enemy
      against my flesh?
Monotonous devil.

Ma formicola – si avvede –
il mondo di patimenti,
il suo supplizio non è suo,
è della specie che si agita
e sciaguatta
        dentro la luminescente vasca.
Oh non lo mortifica,
anzi lo riconforta
la promiscua comunanza.
Quasi non ha più strazio
        nè gloria
il dardo ultimo che lo trapassa.

But he realizes
that the world teems with hurt,
his torment is not his,
it is that of the species
that trashes and swashes
                    inside the luminescent tub.
Oh, the promiscuous sharing
does not mortify him,
instead it comforts him.
The last arrow that transfixes him
        carries almost no more agony
or glory.

Si approssima Firenze.

                    Si aggrega la città.

S'addensano i suoi prima

rari sparpagliati borghi.

                    S'infittiscono

gli orti e i monasteri.

Lo attrae nel suo gomitolo,

                ma è incerto

se sfidarne il labirinto

o tenersi alla proda, non varcare il ponte.

Il seguito è sfinito. Il sonno e il caldo

             ne annientano il respiro.

È là, lei, la Gran Villa

che brulica e formicola.

Di là dal fiume. Lo tenta

e lo respinge,

ostica, non sa

bene in che cosa, ma ostica

eppure seducente,

vivida. In molti lo conoscono,

alcuni tra i Maestri

pregiano, la sua arte,

ma lui teme la loro,

evita il paragone,

Florence is getting near.

               The city gathers.

Its suburbs, rare and scattered just a while ago,

begin to thicken.

            Orchards and monasteries

grow dense.

She draws him into her skein,

               but he is uncertain

whether to brave her labyrinth

or to keep on the bank, without crossing the bridge.

The retinue is exhausted. Sleep and heat

           annihilate their breath.

She is there, the Great City,

teeming and swarming.

Beyond the river. She tempts him

and repels him,

harsh, he doesn't really

know in what, but harsh

and yet seductive,

vivid. There are many who know him,

some of the Masters

value his art,

but he is afraid of theirs,

he avoids the comparison,

non desidera il confronto.
Lo soppiantano – si dice –
Avverte il mutamento. Subentrano
più rudi,
più solidi e corposi
e prossimi ai mercanti,
è vero, i nuovi artisti.
Irridono la sua sublimità
e quella dei maggiori.
A lui piace e non piace quel vigore
dei corpi, quella forte
passione delle forme.
Non è alto cifrato quello stigma.
Ma questo è ora il secolo, si lascia
alle spalle non lui forse
ma gli umili compagni
nella inarrivabile officina, i «candidi
e celesti fabbricanti
d'immagini» – li chiamano questi,
        fieri del loro nuovo stile.
Ah Firenze, Firenze. Sonnecchiano
intontiti i viaggiatori nella sosta.
Meglio rimettersi in cammino,
prendere la via di Siena, immantinente.

doesn't want the matchup.
He heard they are replacing him.
He notices the change. The new artists
moving in are coarser,
more solid and full-bodied,
and close to the merchants, it's true.
They laugh at his sublimity
and at that of the great ones.
He only half likes
the vigor of those bodies,
that strong passion of forms.
That stigma is not highly stylized.
But this is the century now, it leaves
behind not him perhaps,
but the humble companions
in the unreachable workshop, the "candid
and heavenly makers
of images" – as these call them,
                    proud of their new style.
Ah, Florence, Florence. Dazed, the wayfarers
doze off during their stop.
Better set off again,
take the road to Siena, right away.

Perché ti crucci?

                        indovina

la sua malinconia

– lo sente – il mutismo di Giovanna

e l'uggia nel volto del fratello

la rispecchia,

                    ripercossa

gli si aggrava nel sangue,

gli annebbia la mente.

Eh noi artisti…

siamo soggetti noi artisti a molte umiliazioni,

ci toccano durezze,

arbitri di potenti, ottusità della gente.

Ci viene data con l'arte anche quella pazienza.

L'umiltà del mestiere non ha mai lasciato Ambrogio

o Duccio e nemmeno Cimabue né Giotto.

Perché oggi mi sgomento?

perché la bruta forza

del tempo è inesorabile? per questo?

Non è un errore né un torto,

è una legge, non è perdonata né perdona –

sentenziano con la loro ombra

gli occhi lontani di Giovanna e quelli

                accidiosi di Donato.

Why are you troubled?
                    Giovanna's muteness
guesses his melancholy
– he feels it –
and the annoyance in his brother's face
reflects it,
        thrown back at him
it worsens in his blood,
it clouds his mind
Ah, we artists…
we artists are subject to many humiliations,
we have to face hardships,
the whims of the powerful, the obtuseness of people.
Even that patience is given to us with art.
The humility of the trade has never left Ambrogio
or Duccio or even Cimabue or Giotto.
Why am I dispirited today?
because the brute force
of time is inexorable? is that why?
It is neither a mistake nor a wrong,
it is a law, it is not forgiven nor does it forgive –
Giovanna's distant eyes and Donato's shiftless ones
pass judgment with their shadow.

L'incubo, il rivale

M'incalza egli alle spalle, mi tampina.
La sua ombra entra nella mia,
progressivamente la sovrasta,
la ingloba, se l'appropria –
                                        massa
d'oscurità che insieme produciamo
percorrendo quel lembo
di città, in quel momento,
sotto quella obliqua vampa –
nembo che poi si sbiocca,
si sfilaccia, si dissolve
entrando noi ciascuno dentro la propria notte
nella sua agonia, nella sua grazia
verso lo stesso termine, l'alba.
Oh quante vie per una sola meta.
Quanti virgulti per una sola fiamma.

The Nightmare, the Rival

He presses me from behind, he stalks me.
His shadow enters mine,
little by little it hangs over it,
absorbs it, makes it part of itself –
                a mass
of darkness that we produce together
walking across that edge
of the city, at that moment
under that slanting flame –
a nimbus that then flakes off,
frays, dissolves
as each of us reenters his own night,
his own anguish, his own grace
toward the same end, the dawn.
Oh, how many roads to reach one goal.
How many shoots for one blaze only.

Nel ricordo o nel presente?
Entra, sera di sole,
sera estrema di solstizio
nel costato di Firenze,
ne infila obliquamente
i tagli, le fenditure,
ne infiamma le ferite,
le croste, le cicatrici,
ne infervora le croci,
le insanguina copiosamente.
Lui controcorrente
si trascina la sua ombra
verso quella sorgente.
In fronte gli si scheggiano le linee,
gli si disfanno le moli,
gli si frantumano i tetti
sopra una polverizzata gente.
Risale lo sfacelo,
scansa quelle macerie
di una ancora
                    non cancellata
e non assolta storia,
voglioso di primizia,
avido di semenze.
Non empio, non ingordo,
servo della vita – e basta.

256

In memory or in the present?
The evening of sun,
last evening of the solstice,
enters Florence's ribcage,
it slips obliquely
in her cuts, her crevices,
it inflames her wounds,
her crusts, her scars,
it makes them bleed profusely.
He drags his shadow
against the current
toward that spring.
The lines splinter before him,
the masses fall apart,
the roofs shatter
above the pulverized people.
He climbs up that devastation again,
avoids those ruins
of a history
      not yet erased
or absolved,
wanting the first fruit,
eager for seeds.
Not cruel, not greedy,
life's servant – and nothing else.

Discese su Firenze una triste sera.
Oppure trasalì dalle sue pietre,
entrò dalle sue porte?

                    Non conobbe

la mente

        e neppure il profondo cuore seppe
il perché di quella pena,

                    si smarrì

nella penombra
di quel non rassegnato dopomorte –
oscuro controcanto
di che gioiosa epoca? o rimorso
per il suo interminabile
rodio di purgatorio.

A sad evening descended upon Florence.
Or maybe it rose up from among her stones,
entered from her doors?

                    The mind

never knew

               nor did the deep heart find out
the reason for that pain,

          it got lost
in the half-shadow
of that unresigned afterdeath –
dark countermelody
of what joyous epoch? or remorse
for its endless
purgatorial gnawing.

Pietre, aria, il chiaro rudimento,
la tenera balbuzie
di un eloquio – quale eloquio
                         fermo
al purissimo alfabeto
non ancora umano,
nell'intonso libro,
nel celestiale orizzonte…
                         Su quello
come nuvole
            sarebbero
    con le loro ombre
passati gli uomini –
                    più avanti accovacciata
                    o stesa nei ripari,
altrove abbarbicata
al sole e alla frescura,
stanziata alla sorgente,
al seguito o in corteggio
                         quella
moltitudine animale,
                    altra in transito
                         stupefatta
fino a che punto sia

Stones, air, the clear rudiment,
the tender stutter
of a speech – what speech
                    still rooted
in the purest alphabet
not yet human,
in the unshorn book,
in the heavenly horizon…
                    Like clouds,
men would pass
                    over it
with their shadows –
                    further on crouching
                    or lying in the shelters,
elsewhere clinging
to the sun and the coolness,
stationed at the spring,
in the retinue or the following
                    that
animal multitude,
                    and another still in transit
                              astonished
at how deep the day

entrato nella selva il giorno…

L'avrebbero poi lasciata
vergine dietro sé,
     intatta,
       fiato, vento, respiro
       della natura…
           Ma chi

  viene che si radica,
s'impianta con tutta la sua forza
e scende al sottosuolo
e penetra la zolla
        sanguificando
il pianeta
     d'umanità
        e di dolore?
           Chi è

non lo sappiamo
se non da insanabile rimorso –
così tutti lo siamo,
tutti universalmente
quel corpo disseminato,
profuso, ricomposto
in compagine-unità
dalla sola sofferenza…

has come into the forest…

They would then leave it
virginal behind them, intact,
                    breath, wind, stir
                    of nature…
                              But who
        comes and grows roots,
gets entrenched with all his strength
and descends into the ground
and penetrates the sod
                    bloodying
the planet
        with humanity
                    and pain?
                              We don't know

who he is
except through an incurable remorse –
so are we all
all universally
that strewn body,
profuse, recomposed
in wholeness-unity
by suffering alone…

Ma ora obnubilati
ora usciti dal nembo
quasi sfolgoranti soli
andiamo su e giù
nel tempo, tempo noi stessi
nell'immateriale acquario
dimentichi del sangue,
dimentichi d'alleanza e amalgama
alla cieca, per abbaglio
ponendo nel futuro
i segni d'un'antica prova, i semi
d'avvenire nella defunta epoca…
Oppure non ha tempo il tempo,
non ha tempo la mente
umana e la sua brace.

But at times beclouded
at times out of the nimbus
almost blazing suns
we go up and down
in time, we ourselves time
in the immaterial aquarium
mindless of blood,
blindly mindless of the alliance
and the amalgam, deluded
into placing in the future
the signs of an ancient trial, the seeds
of time to come in the dead epoch…
Or maybe time has no time,
no time the human mind
and its embers.

Ma ora s'ammanta
di tutto l'azzurro
lei, fanciulla. S'introna,
s'inaugusta
di limpida maestà.
                    Subito
a lei si affronta
ma da più alto luogo,
alata, una figura.
È l'angelo, è l'annunzio.
S'incendia l'aria, il visibile.
                    Giovanna nella calura si assopisce.
Oh lui dipingerà: dopo, nel tempo giusto.

But now the young girl
is all enveloped by blue.
She sits on the throne,
she becomes august
with simple majesty.

              Suddenly
a winged figure
appears before her,
but from a higher place.
It is the angel, the announcement.
The air, the visible catch fire.

              In the heat Giovanna dozes off.
Oh, he will paint: later, when the time is right.

Non chiederle altro –
sia lei quella che è,

                    mattina fulgida
mattina di luglio,

                    ancora un po' aquitante,
già prossima al cristallo
gioioso in cui s'invitria
sì, ma solo quel tanto… Mattina
effimera, eppure unica al mondo,
universo spazio, universo tempo…
Demorde ora il rimorso
la sua imprendibile sostanza,
tutto ciò che eternamente manca
traversa il mare della sua mancanza,
viene, colma l'assenza.
Si ricompone il mondo, si unisce
per compiermi oppure per trafiggermi? –
ancora lui rapito
puerile, puerile si domanda.

Don't ask anything else of it –
let it be what it is,
                    July morning,
brilliant morning
                    still a bit watery,
already close to the joyous
crystal in which it glazes,
but only so much… Ephemeral
morning, and yet unique in the world,
space universe, time universe…
Now remorse gives up
its unseizable substance,
everything that is eternally absent
crosses the sea of its nonpresence,
 it comes, it fills the absence.
The world recomposes, it reunites
to complete me or transfix me?   –
still rapt,
he childishly, childishly wonders.

Esce dalle riserve,
entra nella sua giornata il male,
entrano nella loro
                    il buono ed il benefico
del mondo, della vita.
                    Camminano
egualmente verso il cuore
delle loro ore prossime il nascente
ed il morente,
                    aumentano
ad ogni nuovo istante
il passato di passato
                    ed il futuro
di futuro tempo –
                    ribatte se medesimo,
                    pensiero antico
                    o suo brano, un
                    petulante accento
mentre viene
                    una nell'alba
sonoramente ticchettando
fin sotto la sua stanza
e passa oltre, si estingue,
                    misura di che perpetua danza...

Evil comes out of its reserves,
it enters its day,
                    what's good and beneficial
in the world, in life,
enter theirs.
                    What is being born
and what is dying walk
equally toward the heart
of their coming hours,
        at every new instant
the past grows in past time
        and the future
in future –
                    ancient thought
                    or its shred, a
                    petulant accent
                    repeats itself
while in the dawn
a measure of what perpetual dance
comes loudly ticktacking
below his room
                    and it goes by, dies out…"

Squillò, luce
di luglio, si disfece
dei suoi velami il monte
dinanzi a lui che cavalcando il muro
sovrastò tutta la conca,
ebbe sotto quell'azzurro
e quella flagranza.
Niente lo richiamò
al suo presente
                    o gli ribatté lo spazio,
il tempo,
        la storia
fino a lui accaduta
e in lui, parve, perenta.
Nessuno lo trattenne
nella sua galoppata
verso dove? l'interno
quasi di un infinito grembo
intentato dalla vita,
eterno, di cui era
lui stesso una indivisa parte
e gli fu beatitudine quel vento
fino alla ricaduta in sé, al tormento.
Prole dell'uomo che mi trafiggi il fianco.

The July light
rang out, the mountain
shed its veils
in front of him who astride the wall
commanded the whole basin,
had that blue
and that fragrance below.
Nothing called him back
to his present
                or threw back space,
time at him,
        the history
that had happened as far as him
and in him, seemed extinguished.
No one held him back
in his gallop
toward where? the interior
almost of an infinite womb
untouched by life
eternal, of which he himself
was an undivided part
and that wind was a bliss to him
until he fell back into himself, toward torment.
Progeny of man that pierces my side.

Pasceva noi, tutto di noi brucava,
                                    sole senza riparo.
Dov'era? – l'anima, intendeva:
sparita nella clandestinità,
perduta? o invece scesa
nell'intima sostanza
dell'ora e delle cose, onnipresente
nel minuzioso agone
sicché non dava nuove
di sé, parlava, muta, da ogni dove
in tutte le ferie,
in tutte le prove? Questo era.
E questo aveva
                    inconsapevolmente
messo da sempre nelle sue bandiere,
issato nei suoi trepidi vessilli
come segno di vittoria.
Fosse conquista o resa – o cielo
                    questo che argomento era?

The sun without shelter
grazed on us, it browsed us completely.
Where was it? – the soul, he meant:
gone into hiding,
lost? or had instead descended
into the intimate substance
of the hour and of things, omnipresent
in the meticulous agon
so that it gave no news
of itself, it spoke, mute, from everywhere
in all the respites,
in all the trials? It was this.
And this he had always
                unconsciously
put in his flags,
hoisted in his quivering banners,
as a sign of victory.
Whether conquest or surrender – heavens,
                what kind of argument was this?

L'universo, i morti. Ne immagina
nell'etere gli opachi
o cristallini insediamenti. *Loro*
dove stanno? – intende i suoi più cari.
Ne issa per un attimo quel vago
sfavillio di firmamento,
                                si sposta
lui, si sposta il desiderio
                                col suo ago
da stella a stella
in tutto il mirifico quadrante,
e qualcuno ne ravvisa
o crede «ma è un'insidia
del rimpianto, quella» il senso
si ravvede. Con esso gioca a volte,
nelle sue perenni ondate
                                l'incessante
loro e nostro mutamento.
                                È vero, è vero
ma persiste il cuore,
                        l'umano non si arrende.

The universe, the dead. He imagines
in the ether their opaque
or crystalline settlements. *They*
are where? – he means his most loved ones.
For a moment he fixes
their faint sparkle in the firmament,

                he moves,

and so does desire

          with its needle

from star to star
in the whole marvelous quadrant,
and he recognizes some of them
or so he thinks "but that is an ambush
of regret" sense
makes amends.
Their and our endless change

          plays with it at times

in its perennial waves.

                It's true, it's true

but the heart persists,

          the human does not give up.

Prima la grazia, poi la forza,
dopo la fioritura, ecco, il rigoglio,
la maturità, la festa –
e già, dentro, il rimorso,
già in crescita l'angustia
che costringe
prima il midollo, poi la scorza.
In breve tempo. Per un nuovo tempo.

First the grace, then the strength,
then the blossoming, there it is, the full bloom,
the ripeness, the feast –
and already, within, the remorse,
already growing is the tightness
that first forces
the marrow, then the bark.
In a short time. For a new time.

Di quel flusso di vita
l'opera appena tratteneva il segno.
Perdeva senso l'opera, certezza
il mio essere stato.
Su quel nulla di fatto scese l'ombra.
Si fece notte. Rifulse
essa, calvaria
dilavata di me
e con me d'ogni
impurità e ogni scoria
di febbre, di turbamento.
Notte vuota, notte plenaria.
Non ero io nel niente,
però. Ero
più ancora nell'essente.

                       Mi pensai

salma spolpata
da piranha celestiali,
                 osso pulito
dall'aridità dei venti –
                di rimorso
di purificazione –
sotto quella luminaria,
                 quando,
quando, Dante,
la rivestita carne alleluiando?

The work barely retained a trace
of that flow of life.
The work was losing sense, certainty
my having been.
Darkness descended on that nothingness.
Night fell. It blazed,
skull cleansed of me
and with me of every
impurity and dross
of fever, of disquiet.
Empty night, plenary night.
I was not in nothingness,
though. I was
rather in being

         I thought of myself
a corpse stripped of flesh
by heavenly piranhas,

         a bone picked clean
by the dryness of the winds –

           of remorse
of purification –
beneath those teeming lights,

        when,

when, Dante,
singing alleluia for the reborn flesh?

LUI, LA SUA ARTE

HE, HIS ART

Dove mi porti, mia arte?
in che remoto
deserto territorio
a un tratto mi sbalestri?

In che paradiso di salute,
di luce e libertà,
arte, per incantesimo mi scorti?

Mia? non è mia questa arte,
    la pratico, la affino,
le apro le riserve
umane di dolore,
              divine me ne appresta
lei di ardore
e di contemplazione
nei cieli in cui m'inoltro…
          Oh mia indecifrabile conditio,
           mia insostenibile incarnazione!

Where are you taking me, my art?
into what remote
deserted territory
are you suddenly thrusting me?

Into what paradise of health,
light and freedom,
art, do you lead me with your spell?

Mine? this art is not mine,
     I practice it, I refine it,
I open the human
reserves of pain to it,
             it readies
divine ones
of ardor and contemplation for me
in the skies in which I advance...
                 Oh my indecipherable *conditio,*
                 my unsustainable incarnation!

Terra ancora lontana, terra arida
graffiata dalla tramontana –
le raspa il mulo
con lo zoccolo l'indurita crosta.

      Passano
su di lei da borgo a borgo,
ricorda, i mercanti in carovana
e i pellegrini verso Roma.

       Passano
talora da castello
a castello in solitudine
sulle loro bardate
cavalcature i capitani
con la mente a Siena
e al suo difficile governo.
Potrò, forse potrò
fissarne il più romito…
e anche lui sarà passato
senza traccia – ah grazia
equanime – su quelle luminose lande,
avendo molto provato e molto dato,
essendo e quasi non essendo stato.

Still distant land, arid land
chafed by the north wind –
The mule rasps its hardened crust
with its hoof.

                        The merchants
and the pilgrims going to Rome
pass over it from town to town
in caravans, he recalls.

                    From castle
to castle in solitude
from time to time the captains pass
on their harnessed mounts
with their mind on Siena
and her difficult government.
I will be able to, maybe I will be able
to capture the most solitary of them…
and he too will have passed
without a trace – oh impartial
grace – over those luminous moors,
having experienced much and given much,
having and almost not having been.

Mi guarda Siena
                    mi guarda sempre
dalla sua lontana altura
o da quella del ricordo –
come naufrago? –
                    come transfuga?
mi lancia incontro
                    la corsa
delle sue colline,
mi sferra in petto quel vento,
lo incrocia con il tempo –
il mio dirottamente
che le si avventa ai fianchi
dal profondo dell'infanzia
e quello dei miei morti
e l'altro d'ogni appena
memorabile esistenza…
                    Siamo ancora
io e lei, lei e io
soli, deserti.
Per un più estremo amore? Certo.

Siena looks at me,
　　　she always looks at me
from her far high ground
or from the one in memory –
as a castaway?
　　　　　　　a deserter?
she hurls the onrush
　　　of her hills
against me,
she lashes at my chest with that wind,
she crosses it with time –
mine uncontrollably
rushing at her flanks
from the depths of my childhood
and that of my dead
and of every just
memorable existence…
　　　　　　We are still,
I and she, she and I
alone, deserted.
For a more ultimate love? Certainly.

Infrapensieri la notte

Il sonno, il nero fiume –
v'immerge la sua tempra
per il fuoco, dell'aurora
che lo, avvamperà, lo spera,
l'indomani –
                Sono oscuri
il turchese ed il carminio
nei vasi e nelle ciotole,
                      li prende
la notte nel suo grembo,
li accomuna a tutta la materia.
Saranno – il pensiero lo tortura
un attimo, lo allarma –
pronti alla chiamata
quando ai vetri si presenta
in avanscoperta l'alba e, dopo,
quando irrompe
e sfolgora sotto la navata
il pieno giorno –
                hanno

Interthoughts in the Night

Sleep, the black river –
he plunges his temper in it
for the dawn's flame
that tomorrow will set him on fire,
he hopes –
                        The turquoise
and the carmine are dark
in the bowls and cups,
                        night
takes them in her womb,
unites them with all matter.
They will be – the thought tortures him
a moment, it alarms him –
ready for the call
when dawn appears in reconnaissance
at the windowpanes and, later,
when it breaks through
and full daylight
blazes under the nave –
                        the colors'

incerta come lui la sorte
i colori o il risveglio
per loro non è in forse,
la luce non li inganna,
non li tradisce? E stanno
nella materia

           o sono
nell'anima i colori? –

              divaga
o entra nel vivo

          la sua mente
nella pausa

         della notte che comincia

             smarrisce
e ritrova i filamenti
dell'arte, della giornata…

               Esce
insieme ai lapislazzuli
l'oro dal suo forziere, sì,

              ma incerto
il miracolo ritarda,
la sua trasmutazione
in luce, in radiosità
gli sarà data piena? Avrà
lui grazia sufficiente
a quella spiritualissima alchimia?

fate is as uncertain as his own,
or the awakening for them
is not in doubt,
the light does not deceive them,
does not betray them? And the colors
lie in matter
               or are they
in the soul? –
                 his mind is sidetracked
or enters the quickening
in the pause
      of the night's outset –
           he loses
and finds again the threads
of art, of the day…
              The gold
does comes out of his strongbox
with the lapis lazuli,
              but the miracle
is held back, uncertain,
will its transmutation
into light, into radiance,
be given to him fully? Will he have
sufficient grace
for that utterly spiritual alchemy?

Si addorme,
s'inabissa,
è sciocco,
lo sente,
quel pensiero, è perfida quell'ansia.
Chi è lui? Tutto gioca con tutto
nella universale danza.

It falls asleep,
it sinks deep,
that thought is foolish,
he feels it,
that anxiety treacherous.
Who is he? Everything plays with everything
in the universal dance?

Arte, cosa m'illumina il tuo sguardo?
la vita o la memoria
della vita? i suoi lampi,
la sua continuità?
del sempiterno fiume l'alveo o il flusso?
Giovanna – la ricordo
in quella lunga sosta
al riparo del carro
stesa supina su un erboso drappo.
Ma che mai riflettevano quegli occhi
incantati dal meriggio: le nuvole?
migranti desideri?
perduti tempi?
                    oppure la costanza
dell'essere, lassù,
                    immobile nell'azzurro campo?
Che cosa rispecchiavano del mondo:
il mutare o il permanere,
l'effimero o il durevole
quelle lucenti spere?
Ma sciocco era distinguere,
                    variavano le parti,
operavano due diverse guise
di un'unica vivente fedeltà
e lei n'era l'immagine,
acqua ed agata, olio e sangue. Amen.

Art, what does your gaze illuminate for me?
life or memory
of life? its flashes,
its continuity?
the bed and flow of the eternal river?
Giovanna – I remember her
in that long stop
sheltered by the wagon
lying on her back on a grassy cloth.
What did those eyes enchanted by the noontide
ever reflect: the clouds?
Migrating desires?
Lost times?
      Or rather the constancy
of being, up there,
                motionless in the blue field?
What did those shining spheres
reflect of the world:
what's changing or enduring
the ephemeral or the lasting?
But making that distinction was foolish,
                the parts varied,
two different forms
of a single living faithfulness were at work
and she was their image,
water and agate, oil and blood. Amen.

Risveglio inquieto, angelica
demonica la ridda
attorno ai suoi pensieri,
no, dentro di essi...

                    Pensiero suo...

                                        facendosi

                    disfa la sua face
                    nella troppa incandescenza.

                    Brucia,

dove lo conduce? È prossima
la vista, ne presente
l'estremo accecamento,
di che ultima fornace –
di tenebra? di lievitante luce?
Ma lei, volto fiorito
sulla grazia dello stelo,
tutto domina, ovale
appena appena
granito porporino,
tutto in sé contiene,
seduta sul suo trono
di pace e di vertigine.

Restless awakening, angelic
demonic the reel
around his thoughts,
no, inside them…

       His thought…

          forming itself
      it undoes its torch
      in the extreme incandescence.
         It burns,
where is it leading him? Near
is the sight, he anticipates
its extreme blinding –
of what last furnace?
of darkness? of leavening light?
But she, face flowering
on the stem's grace,
dominates everything, an oval
just barely
granulating purple,
contains everything in herself,
seated on her throne
of peace and vertigo.

Stasi – morta l'immagine,
a picco, in se medesima. A piombo
caduta la visione,
decomposta in brani,
esatta l'insolazione.
Occhio verde del fiume –
è luglio – tra il fogliame;
vetro pigro-fluente,
verde, verde liquame.
Canne, erba, muschio, fiume,
verderame, verde quasi bitume.
Specchio di chiari cieli,
dov'è radura, di nubi.
Delizia nello stare,
pigrizia nell'andare
dell'acqua, delle creature.
Oh estate, oh minima stazione
d'immensa verità. Nume.

Stasis – the image dead,
straight up, within itself. The vision
has fallen plumb,
fragmented into shreds,
the sunlight is precise.
Green eye of the river –
it's July – amid the foliage;
lazily flowing glass,
green, green mire.
Reeds, moss, river, grass,
copper green, almost bituminous green.
Mirror of clear skies,
where there is a clearing, of clouds.
The water's, the creatures'
delight in staying,
laziness in going.
Oh summer, oh minimal station
of immense truth. Deity.

Pittura, mi mancavi. Infine, eccolo,
è forte, è nell'aria,
lo captano, a uno a uno
i miei sensi magati

          il desiderio

umano, e non umano
dei palmizi e delle dune,
dei cieli e delle rocce,

               delle cose,

tutte, di natura e d'arte
che accompagnano, l'uomo,
ne commentano la sorte –
anelano, è il momento,
a entrare nella spera
della loro vera forma, esse,
ciascuna nella propria
come stelle nel loro firmamento,
ciascuna a dimora nella gemma
del suo colore vero
da materia e essenza.
Io l'accendo. Tutti noi attendiamo
l'avvento della luce

          che ci unifica e ci assolve.

Painting, I missed you. Finally, there,
it's strong, it's in the air,
one by one my bewitched senses capture it,
                    human
and non-human desire
of palm trees and dunes,
of skies and rocks,
                    of the things,
all of them, in nature and art
that accompany man
and comment on his fate –
they long to enter
the sphere of their true form,
the time has come,
each in its own
as stars in their firmament,
each dwelling in the gem
of its true color
from matter and essence.
I ignite it. We all await
the advent of the light
                    that unites us and absolves us.

Stelle alla prima apparizione
               esse, le immagini,
               non meno le parole.

                             Sbocciano

all'orlo in luce dell'estremo niente
appena sopra il baratro
della non conoscenza.
Ne granisce però
nei secoli, vita dopo vita,
forte il senso – oro
di che magnificenza
di frumento, messe di che celeste campo.
Ne crescono altre poi, caotiche,
ordinate in firmamento
a vincere l'incipiente
opacità di quelle, di quelle l'insignificanza.
Fa' che s'apra a ricevere la mente
con gioia e con sgomento
– però senza avarizia
o scemo orgoglio – quell'abbondanza…
Così forse fu sempre
l'arte.

       L'arte meravigliava i suoi maestri.
Non toglietemi mai
da quella vertiginosa danza.

Stars at their first appearance,
$\qquad$ they, the images
$\qquad$ not any less the words.

$\qquad\qquad\qquad$ They bloom

at the lighted edge of extreme nothingness
just above the abyss
of non-knowledge.
But their sense
seeds strongly
across the centuries,
life after life –gold
of what magnificence
of wheat, harvest of what heavenly field.
Then more grow, chaotic,
arranged in the firmament
to conquer the incipient
opacity of those others, their insignificance.
Let the mind be opened to receive
– but without greed
or silly pride – that abundance…
Maybe art was
always so.

$\qquad$ Art amazed its masters.
Never take me out
of that dizzying dance.

E ora lo conduce la vacanza
al cuore antico della sua città
stralunata dalla feria.
                       E lui si perde
– sono io ancora? –
               dall'una all'altra
in quelle stupefatte vie
                   attirato in una rete
d'immaginate e vere sofferenze,
evoca – alcuni ne rivede
con il fiato sospeso
tra memoria e senso –
coloro che accesero con lui
                  di vita quelle alte case
e vi portarono morte,
misero eternità in quelle stanze.
Il tempo, lo sente nella carne,
pieno e vuoto di loro
                     in sé tutto equipara,
però non li elimina,
               di tutta
quella caducità si gloria,
e umilmente la glorifica. Città. Torri.

Now the vacation takes him
to the ancient heart of his city
made frantic by the fair.
                    And he wanders
– is it still me? –
                    from one to the other
of those astonished streets
                    drawn into a web
of imagined and real suffering,
he summons – he sees some of them again
with his breath held still
between memory and sense –
those who with him
                    had kindled the flame
of life in those high houses
and brought death in them,
placed eternity in those rooms.
Time, he feels it in his flesh,
full of them and empty of them
                    makes everything equal
within itself,
but does not eliminate them,
                            it glories
in that fleetingness
and humbly glorifies it. City. Towers.

Nuovi luminosi incanti,
                    nuove
celestiali incandescenze
di senso e desiderio,
                    nuove
a quell'altezza
              insospettate, concretezze
di uomini e d'eventi –
                    così un'epoca
                    d'ardore e d'acrimonia
prodigava i propri istanti
e alcuni s'addensavano
in forme,
          altri infuocavano
l'azzurro
          e la terra di Siena dei dipinti,
altri erano santi –
                    di anno in anno
                    esistenza in esistenza
                    si frangevano i tempi
                    tra quelle terse
                    durature immagini…
questo imparavano gli infanti,
di questo tacevano sgomenti.

New luminous enchantments,
                    new
heavenly incandescence
of sense and desire,
                    new
at that height
                    unsuspected concreteness
of men and events –
                         so an epoch
                         of ardor and acrimony
lavished its moments
and some of them crowded
into forms,
        others inflamed
the blue
        and the sienna of the paintings,
others were sainted –
                    from year to year
                    existence in existence
                    times shattered
                    amongst those terse
                    lasting images…
this is what the children learned,
in dismay they kept silent about this.

Sibilla

A che vi lascio, miei posteri?
            Che ridere, mi chiamano
            strega alcuni, altri
            invece matriarca –
                        interroga,
s'avvede
e n'è meravigliata lei medesima,
che cosa? non già dentro di sé,
                   buia cisterna,
            il deposito del sapere umano,
            la riposta antiveggenza
né caos né caso
né ordine o teoria
di prefigurati eventi
            ma l'essere – risponda
            lui, risponda
            da tutto il suo creato grembo
            ombra e luce generante,
                  il vivido
            che nessun futuro infrange
            e distorna dal suo polo – quale?
            è forse scritto in noi,

Sybil

What do I leave you to, posterity?
                It's laughable, some call
                me a witch, others
                instead a matriarch –

                                she questions,

she realizes it
and she herself is surprised,
what? yet not within herself,
                dark cistern,
                the deposit of human knowledge,
                the concealed foresightedness
neither chaos nor chance
nor order or theory
of prefigured events
                but being – let him
                answer, let him answer
                from his whole created womb
                generating shadow and light,
                                the vividness
                that no future rends
                and diverts from its pole – which?
                perhaps it is written in us,

sciame ignaro vorticante…
                              Ed eccola,
              s'imbianca
                            di tutta la sua età,
                                 la spolpa
l'uso
      immemorabile del mondo.
                              Eccola, non ha sangue,
ha luce nelle vene
                    iniettata dall'aurora
                    diffusa dal mezzogiorno.
È diafana, inesistente.

unknowing whirring swarm…

And there she is,

she whitens

with all her age,

the immemorial

use of the world

strips her of her flesh.

There she is, she has no blood,

she has light in her veins

she is injected by the dawn

diffused by the midday.

She is diaphanous, inexistent.

Si ritira da me lei, mia città,
e io da lei. Finito il tempo dato,
l'amalgama perduto

                oppure. fondono

vissuto e non vissuto
in quel celeste sovrumano tedio
sempre atteso, sempre in agguato…

She withdraws from me, my city,
and I from her. Is the time given over,
the amalgam lost,

          or do lived and not lived
fuse
in that heavenly unearthly tedium
always expected, always in ambush…

Un attimo
di universa compresenza,
di totale evidenza –
entrano le cose
nel pensiero che le pensa, entrano
nel nome che le nomina,
sfolgora la miracolosa coincidenza.
In quell'attimo
– oro e lapislazzulo –
aiutami, Maria, t'inciderò
per la tua gloria,
per la gloria del cielo. Così sia.

A moment
of universal co-presence,
of total evidence –
things go into
the thought that thinks them, they go into
the name that names them,
the miraculous coincidence blazes.
In that moment
– gold and lapis lazuli –
help me, Mary, I will engrave you
for your glory,
for the glory of heaven. Amen.

Rimani dove sei, ti prego,
             così come ti vedo.
Non ritirarti da quella tua immagine,
non involarti ai fermi
lineamenti che ti ho dato
io, solo per obbedienza.
Non lasciare deserti i miei giardini
d'azzurro, di turchese,
        d'oro, di variopinte lacche
dove ti sei insediata
                  e offerta alla pittura
                  e all'adorazione,
non farne una derelitta plaga,
        primavera da cui manchi,
mancando così l'anima,
il fuoco, lo spirito del mondo.
Non fare che la mia opera
ricada su se medesima,
                  diventi vaniloquio, colpa.

Remain where you are, I beg you,
                    as I see you.
Don't withdraw from that image of you,
don't fly away from the firm
lineaments I gave you,
only out of obedience.
Don't leave deserted my gardens
of blue, of turquoise,
          of gold, of variegated lacquers
where you have settled
                    and offered yourself to painting
                    and adoration,
don't make of them a derelict ground,
                    a spring from which you are missing,
so that the soul is missing,
the fire, the spirit of the world.
Don't let my work
fall upon itself
          and become raving, guilt.

Era paradiso, gia'?
Pregava lei, pregava
        ed era
pregata intanto dalla sua preghiera.
Così, fiore crescente,
le si apriva in nuovi sensi,
così le straripava in incrementi
di forza la divinità – era il mondo
sia passato, sia atteso,
sia presente da sempre
a sempre nella sua natività.
Ecco riconosceva dette
        e scritte
dovunque in trasparenza
           verità
credute mute –
lo erano per l'uomo
e il suo buio intendimento.
ma ora? dilagavano
senza riparo di menzogna,
di ottusità. Magnificabo.
    Magnificabo te.

Was it paradise, already?
She was praying, praying,
        and at the same time
was being prayed by her prayer.
So, growing flower,
it opened to her in new senses,
so it brimmed over in increments
of strength and divinity – it was the world
past, awaited,
present, from ever
to ever in its nativity.
Now she recognized truths
believed mute
                said
and written everywhere
in transparency –
they were for man
and his dark understanding.
but now? they were flooding
without the refuge of a lie,
of obtuseness. Magnificabo.

        Magnificabo te.

Scritto, sì, ma in quale
impercettibile scrittura
                    era quell'alfabeto?
                    ne scriveva
lui per luci
ed immagini una parte,
ne magnificava in oro, azzurro,
carminio l'umiltà, il fulgore,
è vero, ma non ne decifrava
punto il senso, intatto traversava
la sua opera il mistero. Arte, oh arte!

Written, yes, but in what
imperceptible writing

             was that alphabet?

             he wrote

a part of it
through lights and images,
he exalted its humility, its brilliance
in gold, blue, carmine,
it's true, but did not decipher
in the least its sense, the mystery
went through his work intact. Art, oh art!

Punto estremo.

        Nessun punto più alto,

                né

di più aspra

      e diamantina tempra.

Non può,

      oltre, andare

né da esso

      recedere la mente.

O così ti pare.

E intanto muta

tutto – e anche tu –

in se stesso: e mutuamente.

Extreme point.
    No point higher,
            nor
of harder
    more adamantine temper.
The mind
    cannot go beyond,
nor recede
    from it.
Or so it seems to you.
And meanwhile everything
changes – you as well –
into itself: and mutually.

In quale punto

                la separazione è posta?

in quale freme?

di me dai miei colori,

dell'arte che fu mia

da me, dai miei problemi?

Gioiosa libertà che aspetti

di là dalle regole osservate

noi artisti, e anche la nostra opera.

Freschissima ritorna in mente Dei

essa, noi nel vago.

In which point
                    is separation placed?
in which does it quiver?
of me from my colors,
of the art that was mine
from me, my problems?
Joyous freedom that might await
us artists
beyond the observed rules,
and our work as well.
It returns utterly fresh in mente Dei,
we into vagueness.

Ti perdo, ti rintraccio,
ti perdo ancora, mio luogo,
non arrivo a te.

           Vanisce
       nel celeste
      della sua distanza
Siena, si ritira nel suo nome,
s'interna nell'idea di sé, si brucia
nella propria essenza
e io con lei in equità,

              perduto
alla sua e alla mia storia…

                Oh unica
suprema purità… Oh beatitudo.

I lose you, I track you down,
I lose you again, my place,
I do not reach you.
                    Siena
        disappears
in the skyblue
of her distance, she withdraws from her name,
she buries herself in the idea of herself, she burns
in her own essence
and I with her equally,
                    lost
to her history and mine…
                    Oh sole
supreme purity… Oh beatitudo.

Estrema sua vecchiezza

                      o un'incipiente

divina gratuità lo invade

vena dopo vena

fino alla sua cima?

Si lanciano come da una torre

al largo i desideri. Svagano

gioiosamente nell'aperto

essi , non è grazia per loro

il pieno adempimento. Non lo vogliono

infatti, non lo cercano

il termine, l'approdo,

il nido. Si diffondono

vibranti del vigore loro

in tutto il luminoso spazio

                 umano ed extraumano

liberi da causa, forse,

perché tutto è causa e insondabile il principio.

Does his extreme old age
        or an incipient
divine bounty invade him
to his peak?
Desires fling themselves into open space
as if from a tower. They wander
joyously in the air,
for them fulfilment is not grace. They do not want it,
in fact, do not look
for the end, the landing,
the nest. They spread
vibrating with their vigor
throughout the whole luminous
        human and extrahuman space
free from cause, perhaps,
for everything is cause and the origin unfathomable.

INTERMEZZO

INTERLUDE

Seme

Minuscolo.
        Minuscolo e invisibile
lui seme
        che affonda
calcato da zoccoli
e da ruspe,
                gli slitta
                intorno
sguisciando la fanghiglia
                            e lui
cala fin dove
            quel limo si rapprende.
È lì la sua dimora,
                eppure
al sicuro non si sente,
                    occultandosi
difende
        da chi?
                la sua minuzia
e la sua incalcolabile potenza.
                            Infila spesso
il merlo invernale

Seed

Minute.
>Minute and indivisible
he seed
>that sinks
trampled by hooves
and scraper blades,
>>the soft mud
slides around him
slipping
>and he
descends down to where
>the mire sets.
There is his home,
>and yet
he doesn't feel safe,
from whom
>does he defend
by hiding?
>his minuteness
and his incalculable power.
>The winter blackbird
often slips his beak
into the crust,

il becco nella crosta,
la disfa, taluno ne scoperchia,
taluno ne piglia,
e spesso si avvicinano nel buio
roditori sotterranei.
No, non c'è pace
d'inverno e di letargo
in quella dimora,
la insidiano la fame
        gioiosa e rabbiosa
          degli uccelli
e l'ingordigia dei topi –
vorrebbe soddisfarli
           lui ma deve
custodire la promessa del domani.
Deve, lo sa, scoppiare,
marcire e trasalire
nel rigoglio.
– Qual è la mano
che ha gettato la sementa?
e lui è dentro it solco
o caduto casualmente
e sperso? – non c'è differenza,
comanda la necessità,
morire e dar nascimento.

breaks it, it uncovers a few
and takes a few,
and underground rodents
often get close in the dark.
No, there is no peace
of winter and hibernation
in that place,
it is threatened by the joyous
                and raging hunger
                        of the birds
and the gluttony of mice –
he would like to satisfy them
                but he must
guard the promise of tomorrow.
He knows he must explode,
rot and burst forth
in that bloom.
– Which is the hand
that dropped the seed?
and is he inside the furrow
or did he fall by chance
and is now lost? – there is no difference,
necessity commands,
to die and to give birth.

È umile, trattiene
quasi timoroso il fiato
l'anno nel suo cominciamento,
sta sospeso, esita
sopra se stesso it mondo,
vige un intimo
raccoglimento di tutte le sue forze
tra la palta e l'acqua,
         l'acqua e gli astri.
Lui ne è al centro,
all'apogeo della sua umiltà,
al sommo del suo servizio,
già prossimo, già pronto
al fato che gli impende,
niente glielo nasconde
it suo prescritto sacrificio, niente –
Ci pensa.
    e già sente

        spigare
        da sé it prossimo frumento,
        il campo oro-meriggio,
oh dolore, oh felicità.
Chi vive questo? chi pensa?
È mente umana
        o universa vigilanza

The year is humble, it holds
its breath almost afraid,
it stays suspended
in its beginning, the world
hesitates above itself,
there is an intimate
gathering of all its strength
between mud and water,

      water and stars.
He is at the heart of it,
at the apogee of his humility,
at the height of his service,
already near, already set
for his impending fate,
nothing hides
his prescribed sacrifice from him, nothing –
He thinks about it

      and already feels

           the coming wheat,

           the noon-gold field

           spiking from him,
oh pain, oh happiness.
Who is living this? Who is thinking?
Is it a human mind

      or universal vigilance

quella che lo accompagna
nella sua agonia
                    o una più vasta
scienza? – ne è,
corpuscolo, una parte
lui e tutto l'altro ugualmente
nella sua esuberanza –
da dove si spicca questo canto
pari a se medesimo
in cui muore la metafora,
muore infinitamente.
Chi ordina? chi parla?
Non ha importanza chi sia
l'autore della vita,
la vita è anche il proprio autore.
                              La vita è.

that accompanies him
in his agony
      or a vaster
knowledge? – he is,
corpuscle, a part of it
and all the rest equally
in its exuberance –
from where does this song take flight
similar to things
in which metaphor dies,
dies infinitely?
Who ordains? who speaks?
It doesn't matter who is
the author of life,
life is its own author also.
                Life is.

Ed ecco, gli viene meno
il suo vigore, lo lascia
un indeciso

          accumularsi
di materia viva, lo svuota
della sua, prende a radicarsi
al suolo, cresce, si erge
già tubero, già bulbo,
già stelo primissimogemmante.
Lo aspettano, lo sente,
le stagioni, non può mancare,

                     è scritto

nel calcolo dei giorni
avvenire il suo tributo.
Leggibile, esso, come vita
e parimente come morte:

                 pari

incrociano
in lui la loro croce
le due, le sole: vita e morte, morte e vita.

Oh gloria, oh dura oscurità
del gran lavoro fatto.

And now his vigor
is failing, an undecided
  mass
of living matter leaves him, empties him
of his own, starts to take root
in the soil, it grows, it rises
already tuber, already bulb,
already firstbudding stem.
The seasons, he feels it,
are waiting for him, he can't be absent,
     his tribute
 is written in the calculations
of the days.
Readable as life
and equally as death:
  equally
the two, the only ones, life and death, death and life
cross
their cross in him.

Oh glory, oh hard darkness
of the great work done.

ESTUDIANT (II)

PEREGRINAZIONI, MEMORIE

ESTUDIANT (II)

PEREGRINATIONS, MEMORIES

Notte, notte dalmatica
trasalita in brividi.
Notte viva, notte emula...
di che? forse del suo medesimo
astrale facimento.
Pullula di tutte le sue luci,
sfavilla sormontando
se stessa vetta sopra vetta
l'infaticabile torrita.
                    Poi s'abbuia
lei o il suo ricordo...
e allunga l'infuocato polpo
le sue branchie, distende
nella nera cavità
del cielo il glome
le sue ariste, s'avventa
                    dalla nera
plaga la tigre dei colori
contro noi,
                    ci gioca,
bambini senza tempo,
si estingue nella rappresentazione
la mirifica commedia.

Night, Dalmatian night
startled into shivers.
Living night, night that emulates…
what? perhaps its own
astral making.
The tireless line of towers
teems with all its lights,
it sparkles surmounting
itself peak upon peak.
                    Then it
or its memory darkens…
and the flaming octopus
extends its tentacles, the kernel
stretches its awns
into the black cavity
of the sky, the tiger
        of colors
lunges against us
from the blackness,
                    the wondrous comedy
plays with us, timeless children,
it dies in the performance.

Non tutto, molto
       però, anima, materia,
              si riprende
il tempo nella sua fucina, a nuove
              necessitudini lo lima.
Qualcosa nondimeno
rimane a se medesimo,
non muore, non declina…
sì eppure a quale fine – anela
il grande anelito –
se in altro non tracima?
                 Oh lo farà,
niente, solo l'inferno
è al bando del mutamento,
murato nell'immobilità.
Niente, questo lo sa.

Not everything, but
     much, soul, matter,
          the world
takes back into its forge, it hones all of it
to new necessities.
Something nevertheless
is left to itself,
that does not die,
does not decline…
yes, but to what end – the great yearning
yearns –
if it does not overflow
into something else?
          Oh it will,
nothing, only hell
is banished from change,
walled in immobility.
Nothing, this he knows.

Chiara
     di luce azzurra
          circea
               quella ultima vacanza.
Si ara, si pettina,
          si struscia
contro sé
stesso il mare
          pizzicato dall'aria,
               mordicchiato
dal vento nella verde-azzurra pelle.
Dura e felice prigionia
dell'uomo nell'umanità,
               tu quanto
gli somigli – ronfa
fatto marino
lui in quel fuoco,
          lui in quel letargo…
               e già
gli ride in mente l'assempro,
gli scoppia in petto il tripudio
di quella
          universa parità
del mondo, del suo cosmo.

That last vacation
was clear
    with blue
        Circean light.
The sea pinched by the air
        plows and combs itself,
        it rubs
against itself,
        nibbled
by the wind on its green-blue skin.
Hard and happy confinement
of man in humanity,
    how much you
resemble it – he snorts,
made sea-like
in that fire,
    in that lethargy…
        and already
the resemblance laughs in his mind,
the rejoicing of that
    universal parity
of the world, of his cosmos
explodes in his breast.

Ne spiccia,

ne deliba

la troppo

incandescente ilarità. O grazia!

He decants
he savors
        its too
incandescent merriment. Oh grace!

È il lampo,

        inaspettato

il tuono. E dopo
allunga verso noi
l'inane
delle sue smaglianti chele,
si approssima, ci afferra
quasi; ma, ecco, si frantuma
in una spiovente gemmeria
l'artiglio d'aria
d'incanto e di paura
della festa, della sera.
È questo nel tuo sguardo –

        o era?

O ancora si rifiuta
in te qualcosa
a quale sfavillio?
Sfugge a quale tenaglia,
si ruba a quale morsa
d'insidia, di meraviglia?
Ma tutto si consuma
in sé, materia
e arte, materia e fede
in questa trasmutante spera.

It's lightning,
        the thunder
is unexpected. And then
it extends
its glowing
immaterial nippers towards us, it gets near,
it almost grabs ut; but suddenly
the airy claw
of enchantment and pause
of the feast, of the evening
shatters
into a streaming gemfall.
Is this in your gaze –
        or was?
Or something in you
is still rejecting
what glimmer?
It escapes what pincers,
it steals itself from what vise
of deceit, of wonder?
But everything is consumed
in itself, matter
and art, matter and faith
in this transmuting sphere.

Riappare – e non è né passato
né presente –
                    l'argento
d'una indimenticata pioggia
laggiù dove l'Italia
                    affonda nel mare la sua punta
sottile come un'unghia
e poi scompare,
                    caligine marina
nient'altro, all'orizzonte.
Perché, anima,
                    ti sposi, ora,
                    tutta con le cose
e non sottilizzi
                    e non discerni
tra vero ed apparenza
come usavi
per solo tuo difetto
nel comprendere,
                    per duro accanimento
                    d'intelletto
                    e sue quisquilie
e non conosci tempo
futuro né passato

The silver
of an unforgotten rain
reappears – and it's neither past
nor present –
down there where Italy
                    sinks its tip
thin as a fingernail into the sea
and then vanishes,
                    sea haze
and nothing more, over the horizon.
Soul, why do you
                    unite completely
                    with things now
and do not split hairs
                    and do not discern
between truth and appearance
as you used to
only because of your failure
to understand,
                    of the hard stubbornness
                    of the intellect
                    and its trifles
and do not know time
future or past

ma unico e indiviso
in cui stanno le potenze
ed avvengono gli eventi?
Chi ti ha chiamato a questo? Io forse,
non io, la mia esperienza?

but single and undivided
in which powers reside
and events happen?
Who summoned you to this? I perhaps,
not I, my experience?

S'aggronda l'appennino
in tutte le sue forre.
                    Lei chiude casa,
s'avvia verso il cancello,
nel bosco le sguiscia sotto i piedi
il mare marcio delle foglie.
Addio estate,
                    eppure non si scioglie
da lei quel lungo tempo
di luce e di sgomento;
non muore, non declina,
è vero, lo trasforma
il desiderio
nella sua fucina…
Così disorientata la rifrange
uno specchio frantumato
di memoria repentina. Oh spirito
che ci agiti
                    e dovunque
nei tempi e nei luoghi ci sbalestri.

The Apennines frown
in all their gorges.
      She shuts her house,
walks toward the gate,
in the forest the rotting sea of leaves
slips under her feet.
Farewell summer,
      yet that long time
of light and dismay
does not let go of her;
it does not die, it does not decline,
it's true, desire
transforms it
into its forge…
So disoriented a shattered mirror
of sudden memory
refracts her. Oh spirit
that stir us
      and toss us everywhere
in times and places.

Non ha mente a niente,
          è debole, è demente
lo scaltro che in tempi altri
e lontani dominò la scena
rusticana, governò le cacce,
preparò i falconi
              eppure, eccolo, segue
con l'occhio il nibbio e la poiana
e altri uccelli alti nell'aria,
ne asseconda con moti
del capo il colpo d'ala
e il colpo di marmaia
del ritmo, ne bilancia
il tempo, il volo, lui creatura
celeste nella sua idiozia,
fatto corda vibratile,
numero, armonia.

The sly one is weak,
        is demented,
his mind is nowhere,
he who in other distant times
dominated the rustic
scene, ran the hunts,
prepared the falcons
                yet, there he is,
he follows with his eyes
the red kite and the buzzard
and other birds high in the air,
he moves his head in sync with their wing strokes
and the axe blow
of the rhythm, he balances
the tempo, the flight, he heavenly
creature in his idiocy,
made quivering string,
number, harmony.

Pilato, secondo Simone

Una pozza di sangue chiuse il conto
del giorno, e dell'«affaire». Non arrivavano
da oltre i monti più precisi indizi.
Di che era l'epilogo? perché
epilogo lo era, di che era
occidente quel crepuscolo?
Si stampò nell'aria, si posò
al suolo gravemente
come un cerbero, come un «hic sunt leones»
quel fulgore porporino.
Sicuro era lo strappo di una perdita,
incerto ma invincibile
lo, strazio, di una travolgente nascita.

Pilate, According to Simone

A pool of blood closed the day's
and the "affaire's" reckoning. No other
more precise sign came from beyond the mountains.
What was this the epilog of? because
it was an epilog, what was that twilight
west of?
That purple glimmer
was imprinted on the air, it settled
on the ground like a cerberus, like a "hic sunt leones."
Certain was the wrench of a loss,
uncertain but invincible
the torment of an overpowering birth.

Scivola giù, sfrascando
lei furtivamente,
foglia moribonda,
si congeda dalle altre.
Un poco ne patiscono il distacco,
un poco si ritemprano
nel verde e nel vigore, esse,
battute dai contrari sensi
del mondo, soggiogate
dal suo inesauribile tormento.

The dying leaf
slides downward stealthily
through the branches,
takes leave of the others.
They suffer her going a little,
they fortify themselves a little
in green and vigor,
beaten by the contrary senses of the world,
conquered by its inexhaustible torment.

ISPEZIONE CELESTE

HEAVENLY INSPECTION

Dinanzi eccole a un tratto
rupi che si disfanno
d'aria e d'oro.

        Le crolla
il giorno,

      l'impero.

          Ne aveva,
– lo ricorda
il sangue, ma appena –
nel luminoso caos

         disceso
all'alba

   e risalito

      i seni,

       trafitto con un grido
l'opaco e il trasparente

         delle aeree valli
poi le era

    tutto il mattino

      divampato
intorno

   luce sopra luce,
radioso, più radioso

      e, dopo, il mezzogiorno

Suddenly ahead
cliffs that crumble
into air and gold.
     The day,
             the dominion
is crumbling before her.
             She had
– the blood
remembers it, but barely –
in the luminous chaos
             of dawn
descended
     and climbed its hollows,
     pierced with a cry
the mist and the transparency
             of the airy valleys
then
     the whole morning
             had burst into flames
around her,
     light over light,
radiant, more radiant
             and, after, noon

le bruciò

       dentro le penne

sangue, nervi,

           le ammollì

tendini

     e acume di pupille

finché si fu incrinata

nell'aria quella tempra

e di nuovo

         si sciolse in libertà

la vita in lei,

       la foga

la riprese

      nel suo celeste gorgo

a lungo

      mentre sempre più un umore

fresco scese

       – un vento – alle midolla

sue e del giorno

divenuto sera

       come ora

che si cala al suolo

         senza pena

e le arriva

      meno vetrosa la cicala.

burned
  blood and nerves
inside her feathers,
    it softened
her tendons
  and the keenness of her pupils
until that temper
cracked in the air
    and life in her
loosened in freedom,
    the ardor
took her back
  in its heavenly vortex
for a long time
  while more and more
a fresh humor – a wind –
    came down to her marrow
and to that of the day
turned into night
  like now
that she dips effortlessly
to the ground
and the cicada
  reaches her less glassy.

Così la notte sale,

         splendore

adesso

    e fine del reame

           o la chiama

lo sfacelo

      a sé,

        a un ultimo

e futuro tripudio

la deflagra –

        o non vale lei

ma il mutamento

in cui vive sovrana

a cui tutta si consacra,

      tutta, fino al suo nulla.

La consuma esso

     eppure non la sperde.

     Non la cancella.

So the night climbs,
                now
splendor
        and end of the realm
                or does
the collapse
        call her
                to itself,
to a last
and future exultation,
it sets her ablaze –
        or it is not she that counts
but the change
in which she lives sovereign
to which she all devotes herself,
                        all, to her nothingness.
It consumes her
                yet does not disperse her.
                It does not erase her.

Riemerge in lontane chiarità
dalle sue latebre azzurre
e grigie, si sveglia,
terra orciana,
alla nostra prima smania
fino alle ultime pendici
                    ed apre
nebulosa
ancora, opalescente
                    la sua oasi
a questa pausa
                della nostra traversata.
Pausa?
        o non lenta
illuminazione
                del torbo e dell'oscuro
del cuore –
            e intanto ascesa
del fragore
chioccio e sordo
                    degli uccelli verso il canto,
il silenzio,
            il canto ancora
                    e il grido di felicità

She reemerges in far-off brightness
from her azure and gray
recesses, she awakens,
Valle dell'Orcia,
to our first longing
as far as the last slopes
                and opens –
nebulous still, opalescent –

                        her oasis

to this pause
        in our crossing.
Pause?
        or not slow
illumination
        of the heart's
mist and darkness –

                and meanwhile the climb
of the hoarse
and hollow din

                of the birds toward song,
silence,
        song again
                and cry of happiness

                              nel colmo
del giorno…
e questo passa
specchiato dalla valle…
                         è lungo
                in opere artigiane,
                                    in mugli
                lontani di motori
                                    sparsi
                in arature,
                            in ozi
                di vegliardi
                          e greggi.
                È lungo, eppure
                su di lei passa,
                              finisce
          se ne va
          il giorno umano
          e non umano,
     le sfugge dall'incavo
     dei suoi piccoli monti,
     si eclissa tra le pieghe
     dei suoi aridi dossi,
                se ne va il giorno
                e l'uomo

                at the height
of the day…
and the day passes
mirrored by the valley…
                it is long
                in craftwork,
                        in distant
                roars of engines
                        scattered
                in the plowing,
                        in the idleness
                of old men
                        and flocks.
                It is long, yet
                it passes over her,
                        the human
                and non-human day
                ends,
                it goes away,
it slips out of the hollow
of her small mountains,
it vanishes among the folds
of her barren peaks,
                day and man
                go away

      e la vita ch'è in loro,
      se ne va
avendo e non avendo
saputo qual è stata la sua parte…
ma è stata – lei lo sa –. È stata
      e questo la fa piangere
talora di grazia e di letizia.

and the life that's in them
goes away
having and not having
known what its part has been…
but it has been – she knows it –. It has been
and this makes her weep
at times with grace and happiness.

Pasqua, ora, nuovamente,
festosa pigolante
negli alberi del mondo,
                    fredda,
                    ruvido-erbata
qui, ma erompe
in chiarità,
            tempra in azzurro
ed ametista
            la lontananza delle sue colline.
Non è fuga quella
laggiù all'orizzonte
e neppure inseguimento. S'apre
a sé risorta
            la terra dopo il gelo
e dopo il travaglio,
si corre incontro, da sé
a sé, si estende in un abbraccio
avido alla sua infinità
o corre in quelle linee
                    l'onda
leggera e travolgente
della resurrezione, si propaga,
trabocca la sua vinta angoscia,
e la riconsacrata sua potenza?

Easter, now, once more,
festive twittering
in the trees of the world,
                              cold,
                    rough-grassy
here, but it erupts
in brightness,
          it tempers in blue
and amethyst
        the distance of her hills.
Down there
on the horizon, that is not flight
or pursuit. The land
opens
          reborn to herself after the frost
and labor,
she runs toward herself, from herself
to herself, she reaches in a greedy
embrace to her infinity
or does the light and overwhelming
                              wave
of resurrection
run in those lines, does her conquered
anguish and her reconsecrated power
brim over?

Brani di tempo e storia –
abdica, tempo stato
per un attimo il presente,
lascia
      al tempo successivo
le sue spoglie
         e sono cibo
esse, sostanziosissimo alimento,
oppure rimasugli,
muffite obsolescenze,
non hanno in sé potenza
alcuna di rigenerazione…
            E devono
con pena
      i posteri sgombrarne
il suolo, pulire l'orizzonte –
ma restano,
      restiamo
noi semi a dimora
a lungo inoperosi
nell'infimo letargo,
        celata
eppure forte
      cova la nostra persistenza
      nell'anno, nel terreno.

Shreds of time and history –
it abdicates, time that has been
the present for a moment,
it leaves
    its remains
to subsequent time
        and they are food,
very substantial nourishment,
or remnants,
moldy obsolescence,
they have no power
of regeneration in themselves…
        And painfully,
posterity has to clear the ground
of them, clean the horizon –
but they remain,
    we seeds
remain bedded
inactive for a long time
in the lowest hibernation,
    hidden
yet strong
    our persistence smolders
    in the year, in the ground.

E quando il principio ricomincia
e s'avviano germoglio e sfacimento,
ecco i tempi si ricongiungono,
colano tutti in una linfa,
svettano in una sola
spigata moltitudine,
che a te corre ventosa, uomo,
a te calda si offre.
                    Oh grazia,
o gratitudine!
                    uomo l'accoglierò,
uomo mi sfamerò
                    di questa
                    e di tutte le mie fami –
dice l'impercettibile bisbiglio.

And when the beginning starts again
and bud and decay set out again,
then times reunite,
they all drip into a lymph,
they rise up in one
spiked multitude,
that runs windy towards you, man,
it offers itself warm to you.

            Oh grace,
o gratitude!

      man, I will accept it,
man, I will appease
           this
           and all my hungers –
says the imperceptible murmur.

Tutto è angustia intorno, tutto
la brutta, la denigra –
mentre s'alza
            nei primi goffi balzi
e tenta i suoi svolazzi
sopra la pesticciata landa.
Disarmonica è la macchina –
lo accusa. C'è pena,
ahi, c'è pesantezza,
                        anchilosi
                    nel mutuo
interagire d'ali, zampe,
tendini, del petto
e della schiena.
Il moto è desiderio.
Desiderio e sofferenza.
Ma questo non la frena,
si ostina lei nel suo conato
infine lancia
la sua spennata massa
nella dritta verticale,
ed ecco ritrova il suo cammino,
risale a ruote ed a volute
un fiume d'aria e d'etere
non sa quando disceso
non sa da chi,

Everything is limit all around, everything
sullies her, denigrates her –
while she rises

           in her firs awkward leaps
and tries her flutters
over the trampled land.
The machine is disharmonic –
she feels it. There is pain,
alas, there is heaviness,

                stiffness
                in the mutual
interaction of the wings, the claws,
the tendons, of chest
and back.
Movement is desire.
Desire and suffering.
But this does not slow her down,
she insists in her attempt
finally she launches
her mass, not fully feathered yet,
in the straight vertical,
and now she finds her way,
a river of air and ether
climbs up in wheels and swirls,
she doesn't know when it descended
or from whom,

       da lei forse

in astrale

      o da altri del suo nido

perduto nella roccia

tra i picchi e i ghiacciai…

      ma ora capovolge

l'ascesa

     i suoi orizzonti

         la spirale

del suo giro

     inverte l'alto

e il basso dei suoi campi,

cala verso l'altura,

       scala

la profondità

     e si cela

a ogni richiamo

nel gorgo azzurro del suo volo. È quella

la sua meta, fine e gioia

del suo moto

quel moto, lo assapora

in tutte le sue piume…

                    perhaps from her
                                    astral body
                    or from others in her nest
lost in the rock
among peaks and glaciers…
                    but now the ascent
upends
        her horizons
                    the spiral
of her circling
                    inverts the high
and low of her fields,
dips toward the hillock,
                    scales
the depths
        and hides
at every call
in the blue vortex of her flight. That is
her goal, end and joy
of her motion
that motion, she savors it
in all her feathers…

E solo per questo era preghiera
                    preghiera vera
non la sua metafora,
per quella sua incertezza
di sé e del suo fine,
per quella felicità, quel bene –
la mente che la abita, la osserva,
la segue, è la medesima,
presente – orante in ogni dove.

And only for this she was prayer
                    true prayer
not its metaphor,
for her uncertainty
of herself and her end,
for that happiness, that good –
the mind that inhabits her, observes her,
follows her, is the same,
present – praying everywhere.

Non girasoli, frumento.
Frumento raso, asportato
in tutta la distesa
di quel seminario,
in tutto il fuoco
di quella tebaide.
Brucia, estate, il suolo
spoglia giro giro
di alberi, di ombre:
poche sparse paglie
se no fulvo cuoiame,
cenere, farina
avara di gramigne.
Brucia, essa, l'aria
e quelle latitudini,
divora l'azzurro
della sua trasparenza.

Siamo qui noi.
Le siamo dentro il cuore.
Ci abita questa ora,
ci colma della sua durata
minuto per minuto
forte, non certo ignara.

Not sunflowers, wheat.
Wheat schythed, removed
in the whole stretch
of that sown hillock
in all the fire
of that wilderness.
Summer burns, she strips
the earth all around
of trees, of shadows:
a few scattered straws
otherwise tawny hides,
ashes, flour
sparing in couchgrass.
She burns the air
and all that vastness,
she devours the blue
of her transparency.

We are here.
We are inside her heart.
This hour inhabits us,
its duration fills us
strongly minute by minute,
certainly not without knowing.

E l'abitiamo noi precisi
come il guscio la mandorla.

Cuoce seme, senno,
cuoce il suo pensiero
nella nostra mente
lei estate piena, estate data.

Poi la notte cala
cerchiata dai monili
di sperdute luminarie,
infine è tutta, nella
forza delle sue stelle,
si chiama e si risponde
dall'uno, all'altro
dei suoi rari cani.
Poi brucia in se medesima,
per domani? per l'eternità.

And we inhabit it as precisely
as the almond its shell.

She scorches seed, sense,
she scorches her thought
in our mind,
full summer, given summer.

The night falls
girded by the jewels
of lost illuminations,
finally she is all in the
strength of her stars,
she calls herself and answers
from one to the other
of her rare dogs.
Then she burns in herself,
for tomorrow? for eternity.

Dove ci sorprende il giorno?
che terre nottetempo
noi acque
del fiume, appena limaccioso
abbiamo attraversato – e ora dove
andiamo, dove
illusoriamente stiamo?
Non è Rodano o Arno
questo incendio,
d'aria e vento
sopra il flusso aperto,

               non è santo
per fulgore d'immagini

                    o rovello
di pensiero e canto
il lume di questa ansa

                    eppure scende
con noi lo stesso lume
con lo stesso sfarzo,
scintilla in queste lande
tra queste solitarie

               nude argille,
lo stesso fondo e celestiale sangue.

Where does the day overtake us?
what lands at night
we waters
of the barely muddy river
have traversed – and where
are we going now, where
illusively are we?
This fire
of air and wind
over the open flux
is not the Rhone or Arno,
        the light of this bend
is not sainted
through the glimmer of images
                            or rage
of thought and song
                    yet the same light
descends with us
with the same splendor,
the same deep heavenly blood
sparkles in these grounds
        amid this bare
solitary clay.

S'accorge il tempo
della sua furtività, tradisce
un soprassalto l'uomo.

               Tempo, l'uomo,

che s'allarma
dentro it tempo fermo,
insediato nella sua durata,
immobile nel suo trascorrimento.
Tempo dell'uomo

              nel paragone con il tempo –

leva esso il suo
pugno d'istanti, d'illusorie
perennità – persi quelli
e queste rapite in quel certame…
ma eccolo, s'infiamma
in cima alla collina,

             lo sfiora

il vento nuovo,

          lui salpa,

           nell'azzurro

e nell'oro si sfarina,
tempo dolente
nella carne, nella storia.

Time realizes
its stealth, a sudden start
betrays man.
                       Time, man,
that gets alarmed
within stilled time
besieged in its duration,
motionless in its flow.
Time of man
                     in the comparison with time –
it raises
its fist of instants, of illusory
perpetuities – those lost
and these swept away in that contest…
but now it catches fire on the hilltop,
                      the new wind grazes it,

it sails, it crumbles
into blue and gold,
time suffering
in the flesh, in history.

S'accovaccia, s'allunga

                oltre la riva

serpente di rossore.

             Nondimeno

sollevano la lenza,

            scagliano

in acqua l'amo

          ancora essi

ostinati pescatori.

Lui, toro mansueto,

le sente, non le cura

nella sua pelle lucente

quelle minime trafitture.

            Va

lui, dimentico delta sua andatura,

perduto nelle sue creature

al cuore chiaro del sapere oscuro.

He crouches, he stretches
                    beyond the bank,
serpent of redness.
            Nevertheless
the stubborn fishermen
still raise the line,
                    throw
the hook in the water.
He, tame bull,
feels those minute piercings
in his skin, but pays no heed.
                    He goes,
forgetful of his pace,
lost in his creatures
in the clear heart of dark knowledge.

È, l'essere. È.
Intero,
inconsumato,
pari a sé.
                    Come é
diviene.
                    Senza fine
infinitamente è
e diviene,
                    diviene
se stesso
altro da sé.
                    Come è
appare.
            Niente
di ciò che è nascosto
lo nasconde.
                    Nessuna
cattività di simbolo
lo tiene
            o altra guaina lo presidia.
                        O vampa!
Tutto senza ombra flagra.
È essenza, avvento, apparenza,

Being is. It is.
Whole,
unconsumed,
equal to itself.
 As it is
it becomes.
 Without end,
it infinitely is
and becomes,
 it becomes
itself
other than itself.
 As it is
it appears.
 Nothing
of what is hidden
hides it.
 No
captivity of symbol
holds it
 or any other sheath garrisons it.
    O flame!
Everything blazes without shadow.
It is essence, advent, appearance,

tutto trasparentissima sostanza.
È forse il paradiso
questo? oppure, luminosa insidia,
un nostro oscuro
ab origine, mai vinto sorriso?

all utterly transparent substance.
Is this paradise
perhaps? or luminous trap,
a smile of ours never conquered,
dark ab origine?

GREEN INTEGER
Pataphysics and Pedantry

Douglas Messerli, *Publisher*

Essays, Manifestos, Statements, Speeches, Maxims,
Epistles, Diaristic Notes, Narratives, Natural Histories,
Poems, Plays, Performances, Ramblings, Revelations
and all such ephemera as may appear necessary
to bring society into a slight tremolo of confusion
and fright at least.

*

Green Integer Books

Green Integer EL-E-PHANT Books (6 x 9 format)